_____

StayLITTMinistries

Stay Living Intentionally To
Transform & Thrive
In Life

A Royal Family
Kingdom Community

Copyright

Embrace Your Kingdom Journey

Copyright© 2024, STAY LITT LLC

All rights reserved STAY LITT LLC

ISBN: 979-8-9909581-1-1

Forward

Inspiring, Thought-Provoking, Challenging, Comforting, Biblical

These are just a few adjectives that describe this incredible 30-day journey.

This journey will help you and me fall deeper in love with the Lord Jesus Christ and challenge us to live out our new identity as Christ followers, or as Ms. Monica would say, "kingdom people." It encourages us to live up to our sacred call by His grace, embracing our identity as beloved children of God.

Ms. Monica guides us on a journey that highlights God's Word as our guidepost for all of life and writes with the beauty and care of someone who has experienced God's transformational power.

Each day, readers will be exposed to excellent expositions of scripture, along with poignant, practical applications that help them integrate the deep truths God reveals through Ms. Monica.

On page 148, she sums up what she hopes readers will take away from this compelling 30-day devotional: "The journey isn't about reaching perfection overnight; it's a process of continual transformation, one where we align our lives more closely with God's love, truth, and grace each day."

I highly recommend this 30-day Devotional Journey. As someone who has served in full-time vocational ministry for over 45 years, I cannot express how grateful I am for the gift of Our Personal 30-Day Journey.

God Bless!

Dr. Dwight A. Perry
Professor of Homiletics and Leadership
Moody Theological Seminary
Chicago, Illinois

Acknowledgement

First and foremost, I am sharing my deepest love, gratitude and thankfulness to Yahweh, God Almighty, My creator, Designer, Lover of my soul, Adonia, Jehovah Jireh, My source, My strength, My Healer, My Daddy. He has blessed me with this mission and his spirit is leading and guiding me throughout this journey of living by faith, obedience, following, growing, listening and doing new things. The journey of drawing near, growing in knowing and loving Yahweh & Yeshua are the foundation of this work, led by his spirit to live for God and share what he guides me to share. My ministry, the Kingdom Journey Guides, my transformation, the renewing of my mind, my new identity and my work to help others to see you properly, learn you accurately, gain their divine identity in Christ and live a joyful abundant life of purpose that reflects you, your Kingdom values and represent you righteously in all we do, think and say as your beloved children, your royal family.

To my beloved, Merciful Gift of God, My son, Myles Nathan... Thank you so much for supporting me, encouraging me, and adding to this work with your input, suggestions, edits, encouragement and being so understanding during this new journey of working, writing and following as God leads me. Your love, support and words keeps me going, in faith, trusting the will and plans from God. You are my blessing, my greatest gift from God.

To my Dad, Ernest M. Griffin, Thank you so much for your encouragement, prayers and numerous conversations that always reminded me to BeYOUnique & follow God in faith. Thank you Dad, for being there throughout this amazing journey.

Table Of Contents

~Introduction, Purpose, Foundation & Overview~

Embrace Your Personal Journey into

God's Kingdom Culture

Welcome to a transformative 30-day journey, designed to deepen your spiritual growth and guide you into Kingdom Living. This journey is more than daily reading; it's an invitation to uncover and embrace God's Word, His Values, Royal treasures and promises, available to you as a child of God. Each day is a step toward understanding your royal identity, aligning with God's values, and stepping confidently into your calling as a Child of God, an ambassador for Christ, reflecting the Kingdom of God in every aspect of your life.

Purpose: Seeking God, Growing Spiritually, and Living in His Kingdom Culture

The purpose of this Journey Guide is to help you grow in knowledge of God's Word, not just as a text but as the living, breathing message of His love, character, and purpose for His children. This journey is about more than learning—it's about being transformed in heart and mind, understanding the depth of God's love as your Abba Father, and knowing your identity as a cherished member of His royal family.

We are intentionally devoting time and coming into each day with an open heart to draw closer to God, seeking to know God through his word and His Holy Spirit, to love him intentionally beyond words, to Love him in our pursuit and obedience.

This is an intentional journey guide to share God's Word, his values and reveal the culture of His Royal Family. This is for renewing your mindset, transforming your mind and ways, building your confidence in knowing the heart, character, faithfulness, love and values of Your Creator, Your Heavenly Father.

This is a journey to see Father God, Learn from our King Brother and embrace your divine identity by walking and practicing the values and ways of God, His Royal Family, The Kingdom Of God. You'll be encouraged to intentionally practice Kingdom values, building a life that reflects God's holiness, wisdom, and grace.

Foundation: Embracing Our Identity in God's Kingdom

As we begin this journey, it's vital to root ourselves in the truth of who we are in God's eyes: beloved members of His family and citizens of His Kingdom. Ephesians 2:19 reveals that we "are no longer strangers and aliens, but fellow citizens with the saints, and are of God's household." This is our identity in Christ—adopted, loved, and welcomed into the royal family of God. Recognizing ourselves as part of this Kingdom changes how we view our lives, our purpose, and the way we live each day. We are not merely individuals going through the motions of religious practice; we are children of the King, chosen to reflect His love, righteousness, and purpose.

Matthew 6:33 directs us to follow King Jesus' words: "Seek first the Kingdom of God and His righteousness, and all these things will be added to you." This call to seek God's Kingdom as our primary pursuit is a powerful reminder that God has not only given us a new identity but a purpose and a path. This journey is about moving beyond routine, beyond simply saying "I am a child of God," to fully embracing what it means to live as members of His Kingdom. It's an invitation to learn, embody, and transform our lives according to the values, principles, and standards of God's divine family.

It's about receiving, accepting and embracing the love, righteousness, faithfulness and adoption into the family of God and citizenship into the Kingdom of God. It's a journey of embracing our royal family identity, authentic care, confidence and love with a distinctive culture and lifestyle.

A Kingdom Lifestyle and culture draws others curiously to the love and light of God. Our growing faith, confidence, royal identity and light shines through how we live, interact, love and engage in the world around us. Our peace, gratitude, joy and our lifestyle are distinct. It's a distinguished Kingdom Cultured Lifestyle that we grow into.

To live as citizens of God's Kingdom is a progressive, submitted journey. It's about opening our hearts to His truth and embracing His wisdom, which leads to a life filled with purpose, joy, provision, protection, community, and fulfillment. As we journey forward, we're embracing a life that mirrors the heart of God and honors our identity as part of His royal family, seeking to live in a way that reflects His love, righteousness, and sovereignty. This journey is a personal adventure into knowing God deeply, growing in His grace, and aligning ourselves with the culture of His Kingdom.

Embracing the Journey: Transformation is a Process Over Time, from the Inside Out.

This 30-day journey is an opportunity to transform your mind, thinking, and daily living by recognizing opportunities and applying the truths of Scripture and the principles of the Kingdom of God into your life. We are growing in knowledge, embracing God's values that transform us for his glory and pleasure for Kingdom Living that cultivates the Kingdom of God Culture. As you seek first the Kingdom of God, you'll discover that everything else indeed falls into divine order, leading to a life of true abundance. If you come across any unfamiliar words along this journey, look them up to increase your knowledge and understanding.

This time that you set aside, prioritize and devote yourself to God's Word is more than a routine; it's more than just reading to read, or checking off that you completed a religious task. This is a journey, an adventure into growing spiritually, gaining accurate knowledge of God, seeing yourself properly and understanding Kingdom culture. The purpose of this journey is about taking our place in His grand design and plan for His Family, taking intentional time to cultivate His values, likeness and image in our hearts, to transform our minds to walk it out in GODfidence and Live it out with confidence in who we are and whose we are.

Start each day with an open heart and sincere prayer, asking God to reveal himself to you, to reveal truth, to give you understanding, wisdom and grace in applying what you learn into how you will live as you are transformed by the renewing of your mind. Ask his Holy Spirit to guide, reveal and teach you as you gain knowledge and insight into the word of God. Ask for the grace to practice what you are learning from God's Word.

As a child of God, you are on a journey of continual learning and growth. It's an intentional **progressive** journey of sanctification and transformation. As you seek the Kingdom of God and pursue truly knowing God our Father and learning Jesus, our King Brother, you will grow in your knowledge, understanding, belief, faith and GODfidence. As you seek God whole heartedly and increase in knowledge, understanding and the wisdom of GOD, you will begin to practice this righteousness. As we practice righteousness and the application of Kingdom Principles, His Holy Spirit will reveal to you, your divine identity as a child of God. You are loved, chosen, redeemed, purposed and empowered. His Holy Spirit empowers you with the fruit to walk and live out our identity and faith. You are called to enter into the Royal Family, The Kingdom of God. All are invited.

A Flexible Path: Embracing Your Own Pace for the Kingdom Journey

This 30-day Kingdom Journey Guide isn't intended to be completed in 30 consecutive days. Rather, it's a guide for intentional reflection, growth, and transformation—designed for you to take your time, allowing each truth to settle into your heart and renew your mind. This journey is about learning God's values, understanding Him as our loving Father, and embracing the principles, standards, and culture of His royal family. It's a time to thoughtfully reflect on His ways and let His truths reshape the way we see Him, ourselves, and the world around us.

The guide encourages you to explore, think deeply, practice what you learn and live out these truths as you cultivate a Kingdom mindset. One suggested approach is to focus on one or two values or themes per week, stretching the journey into about 3 ½ months. This approach allows you to absorb each day's insights through learning, reflecting, and actively practicing Kingdom values in your daily thoughts, actions, and interactions. Each week becomes a time of not just learning but intentionally thinking of God and Practicing the truths revealed in God's word, building the habits that strengthen your identity in Christ and cultivating a Kingdom mindset and culture.

Suggestions for Embracing the Journey:

- **Weekly Focus**: Choose one or two days from the guide each week. Spend the first few days reflecting on the content and the rest of the week intentionally practicing the values introduced.

- **Intentional Application**: As you focus on each day's teaching, look for ways to apply these values in everyday scenarios—whether in your thoughts, relationships, or responses to challenges.

- **Reflect and Journal**: Take time at the end of each week to reflect on what you've learned and the progress you're making. Journaling is a powerful way to track your spiritual growth and see how God's truths are transforming your heart and mind.

- **Stay the Course**: Remember, this journey isn't a race but a pathway to authentic growth. Set a schedule that works for you, but aim to stay consistent. It's through regular engagement that you'll experience the true impact of Kingdom living.

Whether you complete the journey in 60 days, 3 months, or longer, remember that transformation is a process. Take each step at a pace that feels right for you, and embrace this time to deepen your relationship with God, to prioritize fellowship and learning God and Jesus Christ intimately, the shaping of your royal identity, and reflecting the Kingdom culture of our divine family.

Make a commitment to yourself. Schedule the time you will engage. Be honest with yourself and realistic with yourself. Schedule in 20+ mins to engage. Make it your dedicated time to embrace your Soul, your mind, will & emotions. It's your dedicated time to Seek God and Learn with the heart's passion to grow spiritually.

Prioritize time to read, reflect, pray and be still. When you schedule it, you don't need to squeeze it in. If something comes up, you know exactly how and when to get back on your path. Your Life, Spiritual Health & Growth is a priority. Soul Care is essential to our journey of life. Prioritizing our time helps us to be productive and navigate life well.

This is Your Personal Journey, Embrace each day!!!

King Jesus laid the foundation for our Journey

Before we embark on this intentional journey with Day 1, "Understanding Our Place in God's Kingdom," let us ground ourselves in the profound words of the Lord's Prayer from Matthew 6:9-13. This passage not only enriches our prayer life but also deepens our understanding of our adoption as sons and daughters within God's Kingdom.

"Pray, then, in this way:

> 'Our Father, who is in heaven, Hallowed be Your name. Your kingdom come. Your will be done, On earth as it is in heaven. Give us this day our daily bread. And forgive us our debts, as we also have forgiven our debtors. And do not lead us into temptation, but deliver us from evil."

Our King Brother has given us a model to anchor and focus our prayers, our connection and relationship, our daily focus. It fosters a proper view of the Father, How to worship, His purpose, His Plan, Our need for His provisions and reliable keys to Live well as we grow in fellowship and relationship with God.

Let's Get Focused on the Divine Path Before We Begin This Journey:

Our Reverence for God: The prayer begins by honoring God's name, "Our Father in heaven, hallowed be your name." This line reminds us of God's sovereignty and holiness, inviting us to approach Him as father, with reverence due to a King. Have you ever looked up the names of GOD? (Yahweh, Jehovah Jireh, Jehovah Shalom, etc... I encourage you to learn and embrace the essence and attributes of Our Faithful Dependable Heavenly Father) Did you know that God was referred to as father more than 242 times yet he is King.

He is Daddy first, Abba, Our God, Creator, Father then King. Knowing his names, acknowledging him by his names and calling upon him with the names that highlight his attributes as our all powerful father helps us to recognize and pursue an intimate connection and relationship with him as children of the King, that is also our loving faithful intentional Father. (Not a mean, scary God who is always ready to catch you, punish you and condemn you for what you do especially when you miss the mark on a choice or a lesson to be learned) As we learn him and know him accurately, we find our rightful place in His

Kingdom—sons and daughters, experiencing his love, citizens who honor and glorify our sovereign Lord.

The Kingdom Comes: In saying, "Your kingdom come, your will be done, on earth as it is in heaven," we express our intense longing for God's governing values and principles, what he wants for us and what he wants to give us, to be evident in our hearts and lives. This plea signifies our desire to see God's Kingdom values and culture manifested around us, reflecting the harmony and order of heaven in our earthly world. Embracing his ways and values, helps us to be the salt of the world, enhancing lives around us and making our world a better place.

Dependence on Divine Provision: "Give us today our daily bread," acknowledges our dependence on God for all things—both physical and spiritual nourishment. This petition reminds us that our provisions and strength for each day and for fulfilling our Kingdom roles, purpose, assignments and good works are provided by God Himself. This is reinforcing his faithfulness and promise to supply all of our needs, trust and reliance on Him.

Living in Forgiveness: The request, "Forgive us our debts, as we also have forgiven our debtors," emphasizes the importance of mercy within the Kingdom. It calls us to embrace grace and extend forgiveness, just as we are forgiven by our King. This reflects a core Kingdom value, urging us to maintain right relationships with both God and our community.

Seeking Guidance and Protection: Lastly, "Lead us not into temptation, but deliver us from evil" highlights the spiritual realities we face as believers. It is a plea for God's guidance and protection against temptations-the desires we have that causes us harm, steals or destroys. The guidance for challenges and protection from evils that may divert us from our Kingdom path.

As we reflect on these verses, we set the foundation for our intentional devoted journey, preparing ourselves to explore and embrace our place in God's Kingdom. This scriptural grounding invites us to reflect on our identity, our dependence, and our duty within a divine Kingdom order that surpasses our earthly understanding. Let us proceed, with hearts open to learning, growing, and living out the values of the Kingdom under the reign of our Almighty God.

Opening Prayer for Guidance:

Heavenly Father, as I step into this journey, I seek Your wisdom and guidance. Holy Spirit, lead me deeper into the truths of Your Word. Help me to grasp the fullness of my identity as a citizen of Your Kingdom and to live out the principles of Your Kingdom in every aspect of my life. May my faith be strengthened, and may my life reflect Your glory. In Jesus' name, Amen.

As we embark on this intentional journey, let's open our hearts to the transformative power of God's Word and his Holy Spirit. Embrace each day as an opportunity to grow closer to God, to understand His will more clearly, and to live out the reality of His Kingdom here on earth, as his beloved royal Sons and Daughters. We were created, designed and called to be image bears, Children of God for his pleasure, glory and purpose... Embrace Your Journey, Embrace your transformation, Embrace the journey of discovering Truth, his will, righteousness and way... All are invited.

Seek First the Kingdom of God and His Righteousness!

Embrace Your Journey, Embrace Your Royalty

Learn God's Truth, Embrace What He Values

Fellowship and Build an Intimate Relationship

Live What God Values, Experience His Truth

Follow the Way, the Truth and Experience the Life

Experience the Richness of God's Kingdom on Earth

Kingdom Living~ Kingdom Lifestyle~ Kingdom Culture

Day 1: "Understanding First Things First as God's Family"

Leading Scriptures:

- Matthew 6:33 (NASB): "But seek first His kingdom and His righteousness, and all these things will be added to you."

- Ephesians 2:19 (TPT): "So you are not foreigners or guests, but rather you are the children of the city of the Holy ones, with all the rights as family members of the household of God."

An Intentional Pursuit:

In the hustle and bustle of our daily lives, it's easy to lose sight of our true purpose and identity. Yet, the scriptures tell us explicitly and encourages us to a higher calling, one that transcends our earthly worries and aspirations. Matthew 6:33 isn't just a call to prioritize; it's an invitation into a life of divine fulfillment and purpose. When we seek God's kingdom and His righteousness above all else, we align ourselves with His will, opening the doors to His blessings and provisions.

Ephesians 2:19 deepens this understanding by reminding us that our citizenship is not of this world. We are members of God's household, with full rights and privileges. This revelation is profound, urging us to view ourselves and our families not merely as individuals striving for survival but as integral parts of a divine, royal family pursuing Knowledge, relationship and purpose. Our daily lives, therefore, should reflect this noble lineage, access, characterized by love, purpose, and service to God's kingdom.

What does it mean to seek His kingdom in our daily lives? It means to diligently prioritize our time, energy and efforts to pursue, explore, study, understand, learn, consider and meditate on the knowledge of the Kingdom, its principles, secrets revealed and God's righteousness. This is intentional, where daily decisions , action, and thought is considered and filtered through God's values and principles that we discover in our search. It's about recognizing our role, not just as ambassadors of Christ, but heirs, Children called to grow, transform and reflect God in likeness to manifest God's love, wisdom, and justice on earth. This mindset shift transforms how we see ourselves and how we interact with others, our families, our communities, and our world.

Today, let us meditate on these scriptures and ask God to reveal himself to us anew, to reveal to us our unique place within His grand design. As we embrace our identity as His beloved children, let's consider the profound impact of living in accordance with His kingdom values. This is not just about personal transformation outwardly in action but about embracing God and what he has said, from the heart, and taking our place as his chosen beloved children with a part in God's mysterious and glorious plan for all of creation.

Reflect on the benefits of aligning our lives with God's love, promises, purpose, plan and principles. As we seek and embrace God earnestly, he surprisingly gives us the peace that surpasses understanding, joy unspeakable, and the assurance of His unfailing provision and guidance through His Holy Spirit. As we embark on this 30-day journey, let's open our hearts to the transformative power of living as God's royal family, led by His Holy Spirit, dedicated to His will and fulfilling his purpose on earth. **Embrace this journey, You Deserve ALL that God has Reserved. Jesus said he came to give Life, for you to have a better Life , a rich and satisfying life, Life more abundantly. All are invited.**

Question & Reflection:

Think about what you already know about what is written in God's Word regarding his children. How would your life enhance if you received all the promises, provisions and power that God said about his children in his word?

What often gets in the way of you following through to meet your goals? How will you prioritize your time and days differently to invest in your spiritual growth during these 30 days?

Day 2: "Cultivating a Heart of Trust in God"

Leading Scriptures:

- Proverbs 3:5-6 (NASB): "Trust in the Lord with all your heart and do not lean on your own understanding. In all your ways acknowledge Him, and He will make your paths straight."

- Romans 8:28 (TPT): "So we are convinced that every detail of our lives is continually woven together for good, for we are His lovers who have been called to fulfill His designed purpose."

A Willingness to Trust & Embrace Truth:

In the journey of faith, trust is the cornerstone. Today's scriptures invite us into a deeper reliance on God, encouraging us to surrender our understanding and lean into His. Trusting God with every facet of our lives means believing that He holds the blueprint to our destinies and understands our needs better than we do.

Proverbs 3:5-6 teaches us an essential truth: our understanding is limited. Our perspectives are often clouded by our immediate circumstances, fears, traumas and desires. Our past experiences with humans can leave a stain on the lens we view the world and others through. However, God sees the entire picture—past, present, and future. By acknowledging Him in all our ways, we open the door for Him to direct our paths, leading us to outcomes far better than anything we could orchestrate on our own.

Romans 8:28 goes further, assuring us that every detail of our lives, whether seemingly good or bad, is woven together for our ultimate good. This promise is not for everyone indiscriminately but for those who love God and are called according to His purpose. It's a reminder that our lives are not a random series of events but part of a divine tapestry, crafted by the hands of a loving Father.

What does cultivating a heart of trust look like in practical terms? It begins with daily decisions to surrender our worries, plans, and dreams to God, choosing to **believe** in His goodness and sovereignty even when circumstances challenge our faith. It means waking up each day and saying, "God, I may not understand what You're doing, but I trust You." It means trusting him for who he is and not comparing him to what we've experienced from humans. Check out Numbers 23:19 NASB.

Today, let us reflect on areas of our lives where we struggle to trust God. Let's bring these concerns before Him in prayer, asking for the grace to trust Him more deeply. As we do, we'll find our paths straightening, our burdens lifting, and our hearts filling with peace, knowing that we are in the hands of a Father who loves us and is actively working all things together for our good. Remind yourself of the truth. Re-state his words. Tell him what he said. Let his word be the foundation of prayer.

Question & Reflection:

In what area do you struggle to trust God? Is it your finances, health, relationships, future plans, other areas? Why? Now give it to God...Tell him about it, ask him to help you trust him fully because on your own, it may not be possible. Give it all to him and leave it with him.

Day 3: "Living Out Our Identity as Heirs of God's Kingdom"

Leading Scriptures:

- Galatians 4:7 (NASB): "Therefore you are no longer a slave, but a son; and if a son, then an heir through God."

- 1 Peter 2:9 (TPT): "'But you are God's chosen treasure —priests who are kings, a spiritual "nation" set apart as God's devoted ones. He called you out of darkness to experience his marvelous light, and now he claims you as his very own. He did this so that you would broadcast his glorious wonders throughout the world . '

God is our Father first, Embrace your adoption: Our Father, Abba Is King!!! King of the Universe.

Embracing our identity in Christ is foundational to living a life of purpose and fulfillment. The transformation from being slaves to sin and controlled by our flesh to becoming sons and daughters—and thereby heirs—of God's Kingdom is profound. We are the King's Kids. Galatians 4:7

doesn't merely suggest a change in status; it declares a complete overhaul of our identity and inheritance. As heirs, we are entitled to the promises, provision, and power of God's Kingdom. This inheritance includes peace, joy, love, and the authority to overcome the darkness that once held us captive.

1 Peter 2:9 expands on this identity, describing us as God's chosen treasure, priests, and kings. This royal priesthood is not a lofty, unreachable status but a present reality for all who are in Christ. Our priesthood is about our relationship with God and ability to hear from God and receiving His wisdom, insight and instructions. We are set apart, called to illuminate the darkness with His marvelous light. Our lives are meant to be living testimonies of God's grace, mercy, love and power.

Understanding our identity as heirs and royal priests demands a response. It's not enough to acknowledge this truth; we must live it out. This means daily surrendering to God's will, seeking His guidance in every area of our lives, and using our God-given access and authority to bring about change in our families, communities, and beyond. It involves standing firm against the temptations and challenges that come our way, knowing that our identity is secured in Christ. As we live intentionally each day, let us not forget that God is our Father, Our Daddy... We have the first installment of his promises, His Holy Spirit. The Gift of the Holy Spirit is there to guide us. We can go to him, we can depend on him, we can ask him, he is our help. We do not have to figure it all out, acknowledge God, include him, rely on him to guide you and he will lead you in all decisions.

Today, let's meditate on what it means to be an heir of God and a royal priest. Let's ask God to reveal our divine identity, especially the areas where we have not fully embraced our royal identity , to heal from those areas that are still open wounds and to empower us to live out our identity and calling with boldness and confidence.

As we step into this day, let's carry the awareness of our royal heritage with us. Let's live as those who have been called out of darkness into His marvelous light, Kings and Queens, Sons and Daughters of the Most High God. We are the King's Kids. Let's live joyfully with **GODfidence**, the confidence and assurance of truth of whose we are, and ready to share the wonderful deeds of Him who called us his own. This is not just for our benefit but for the glory of God and the advancement of His Kingdom on earth.

Question & Reflection:

How does our identity in God shape the way we view ourselves?

Go beyond what you were told, what people said, what you felt or thought previously. Believe Truth.

How does our identity in God shape the way we view our relationships, and our purpose in life?

Knowing Reading and Embracing Truth, How does our royal identity shape how we will show up and live out loud?

Day 4: "The Power of Our Words: Speaking Life into Our Circumstances"

Leading Scriptures:

- Proverbs 18:21 (NASB): "Death and life are in the power of the tongue, And those who love it will eat its fruit."

- Ephesians 4:29 (TPT): "And never let ugly or hateful words come from your mouth, but instead let your words become beautiful gifts that encourage others; do this by speaking words of grace to help them."

A catalyst for mindsets and creating reality that impacts all who hear:

Our words are powerful tools that can build up or tear down, bless or curse, heal or hurt, calm or stir up. The wisdom of Proverbs 18:21 reminds us of the significant impact our speech has on our lives and the lives of those around us. As bearers of God's image and ambassadors of His Kingdom, the words we speak should reflect His love, truth, and grace.

Ephesians 4:29 takes this concept further by instructing us to use our words as gifts that encourage and edify others. It's not just about avoiding negative speech or not cussing; it's about actively choosing to speak life, offering words of grace that uplift and support. This doesn't mean ignoring reality or pretending that challenges don't exist. Instead, it's about viewing our circumstances through the lens of faith and declaring God's promises over them.

Speaking life begins in the heart. Our words are a reflection of our inner thoughts and beliefs. To speak life consistently, we must first allow God's Word to transform our hearts and minds. This transformation leads to a renewal of our thought patterns, aligning our thoughts with God's truth. When our hearts are full of His Word, our words will naturally flow with life, blessing, and encouragement.

Today, let's be mindful of the words we speak and the words we listen to. Let's challenge ourselves to pause before responding in any conversation, asking the Holy Spirit to guide our words. Whether we're facing a difficult situation, interacting with others, engaging with our family, or speaking about ourselves, let's choose to speak love and life. Let's be intentional about the words we are listening to and feeding ourselves. What we consume in our ears, penetrates our souls and comes out of us. Let's declare God's promises over our circumstances and use our words to build up those around us, including ourself.

Remember, your words can be a beautiful gift to others and a testament to the transformative power of God's grace in your life. Plant his word, water it, bear its fruit.

Question & Reflection:

When things are going good in your life, what do you say?

When things go wrong, what do you say?

The words we use, create the reality we live.

What music are you listening to? What songs are you singing? Who are you listening to?

What are the lyrics saying to you? What words or stories are you feeding your soul?

Reflect on the power of your words today. Ask God to help you see where you might be speaking death instead of life, and commit to making a change.

Day 5: "Embracing God's Peace in a Turbulent World"

Leading Scriptures:

- John 14:27 (NASB): "Peace I leave with you; My peace I give to you; not as the world gives do I give to you. Do not let your heart be troubled, nor let it be fearful."

- Philippians 4:6-7 (TPT): "Don't be pulled in different directions or worried about a thing. Be saturated in prayer throughout each day, offering your faith-filled requests before God with overflowing gratitude. Tell him every detail of your life, then God's wonderful peace that transcends human understanding, will make the guards of your heart and mind through Jesus Christ."

Peace grows with dependency:

In a world filled with uncertainty, fear, and turmoil, the promise of God's peace stands as a beacon of hope. Jesus Himself offers us a peace unlike anything the world can give—a peace that is not dependent on external circumstances but rooted in the eternal, unchanging nature of God.

John 14:27 speaks directly into our anxieties and fears, reminding us that the peace of Christ is a gift, freely given to us. This peace does not ignore the realities of our struggles but offers a tranquility that transcends them. It is a peace that guards our hearts and minds, keeping us steady in the midst of life's storms.

Philippians 4:6-7 outlines the pathway to experiencing this peace: through prayer, supplication with thanksgiving, and presenting our requests to God. This process is not about denying our worries but about surrendering them to the One who is sovereign over all. It's in the act of releasing our control and trusting in God's provision that we find His peace—a peace that surpasses all understanding.

Today, let us practice this surrender. Let's bring our concerns, our fears, and our desires before God, thanking Him for His faithfulness in the past and trusting Him for our future. What can we do by worrying? How many scenarios will we play in our thoughts? If we could do it all, we wouldn't need him. If you continue to read in Philipians 4: on to verses 8-9, we are given keys to keep our mind and be intentional with directing and redirecting our thoughts. As circumstances and life happens, we are able to choose what we focus our thoughts towards. Will it be life or death, positive or negative, worst or best, lovely or detrimental. This is a practice that will grow as you use these keys for peace. He tells us that HE, the God of Peace, *WILL BE WITH YOU.*

Let's practice Depending on God to be God, Trusting God to do as he says, believing that what he said is true. Know that he tells us to cast all our cares on him. Life and living is so heavy when we try to do everything on our own and by ourselves, without God or the help that he sends. This is not the way God leads his family, this is not the way for his children. He is available, reliable, dependable, hearing, concerned and compassionate regarding the things concerning us. He works in us, for us and through us, for each other.

We have this divine opportunity, in your secret place, to have an open intimate conversation, a vulnerable heartfelt release, withholding nothing, confessing and declaring that you will trust him like never before and will be open to his will and his way. End your time by welcoming him into every area of you and thanking him . As we go about our day, let's pay attention to the shift within us as God's peace begins to guard our hearts and minds in Christ Jesus.

Reflect on the areas of your life where you need God's peace. Embrace the peace He offers as you lay down your burdens at His feet. Let today be a day of renewed trust and resting in the presence of God, knowing that He is in control, hears you and that His peace is ours for the taking.

Question & Reflection:

What's worrying you or pulling on you?

What are you holding onto that God is asking you to release to Him?

What makes it challenging to release it and trust God with it?

Tell him... Then leave it there. Give it to God and leave it with him. If it comes back in thought, give it back. Restate the Truth that you know. Remember your words have power. Speak Truth to thoughts that are out of alignment with Truth.

Day 6: "The Power of God's Word in Our Lives"

Leading Scriptures:

- Hebrews 4:12 (NASB): "For the word of God is living and active and sharper than any two-edged sword, and piercing as far as the division of soul and spirit, of both joints and marrow, and able to judge the thoughts and intentions of the heart."

- Psalm 119:105 (TPT): "Truth's shining light guides me in my choices and decisions; the revelation of your word makes my pathway clear."

Consuming to Learn, Grow, Live and Transform:

As we journey through life, seeking direction and understanding, God has not left us without guidance.The transformative power of God's Word is unparalleled. It's not merely a collection of historical documents or wise sayings; it is the living, breathing voice of God that speaks into our lives today. Hebrews 4:12 paints a vivid picture of its penetrating ability—to reach into the very core of our being, discerning our thoughts and motives. This divine discernment is both a comfort and a challenge. It comforts us by assuring that God knows us completely and loves us still. It challenges us by exposing areas of our lives that need change or growth. Even revealing areas that we may have not known were not in alignment with the virtue of God.

Psalm 119:105 highlights another aspect of God's Word: its guiding light. In a world where truth seems subjective and paths seem obscured, the Bible provides clarity and direction. It's a lamp unto our feet, illuminating the step in front of us, even if the full journey isn't visible. This verse reassures us that as we make decisions—big or small—God's Word can guide us toward His will, revealing the right path through its timeless truths.

Embracing God's Word means allowing it to challenge and change us. It requires a heart willing to be molded, a mind open to be renewed, and a spirit eager to follow God's leading. It's about making a daily commitment to read, meditate, and apply the Scriptures in our lives. It's trusting and believing that His word and Holy Spirit has the power to transform us from the inside out.

Today, let's commit to engaging with God's Word more deeply. Whether it's a familiar passage or a new discovery, ask God to speak to you through His Scriptures and to give you understanding and a fresh revelation. Reflect on how it applies to your current situation, your relationships, your challenges, and your decisions. Let's be open to the transformation that comes from encountering God through His Word, allowing it to shape our thoughts, actions, and attitudes. As we do, we'll find our lives aligning more closely with His purposes, and our paths becoming clearer under the guiding light of His truth.

Questions for Reflection and Intentional Transformation:

How can you approach reading God's Word in a way that invites transformation, allowing it to shape not just your understanding but also your actions and attitudes in your daily life?

What areas of your life do you feel God's Word is currently challenging or piercing, and how might you respond to this inner transformation?

Now, take this time to tell God about it. Ask for his help. Ask the Holy Spirit to help you recognize and hear his leading. Then ask for his grace to follow as he reveals to lead you. Sometimes, we can hear or receive instruction yet rationalize why we should or should not follow.

*Sometimes it is our emotions that put our feelings in charge as our leading light on what to do, which goes against the thought or leading that God's Word reveals. Sometimes it comes by doing what you feel in the moment without considering or regard for anything you know as truth. It's when our actions are managed by an emotional feeling or physical sensation. If this is true for you, Ask for insight to the things to cut out of your life that may be blocking you from mentally receiving **and following**. God is faithful and willing. His word will guide as we engage with it and are open to follow as he leads us by his Holy Spirit.*

Day 7: "The Power of God's Word in Transforming Lives"

Leading Scriptures:

- 2 Timothy 3:16-17 (NASB): "All Scripture is inspired by God and beneficial for teaching, for rebuke, for correction, for training in righteousness; so that the man *or woman* of God may be fully capable, equipped for every good work.."

- Romans 12:2 (TPT): "Stop imitating the ideals and opinions of the culture around you, but be inwardly transformed by the Holy Spirit through a total reformation of how you think. This will empower you to discern God's will as you live a beautiful life, satisfying and perfect in his eyes."

His Word is more than a book to read:

As we journey through life, seeking direction and understanding, God has not left us without guidance. The scriptures we hold in our hands are more than just ancient texts; they are the living, breathing Word of God, infused with the power to transform our lives from the inside out. God, our Father never intended for us to live life without his wisdom and guidance. The transformative power of God's Word is unparalleled.

2 Timothy 3:16-17 highlights that God's Word is not merely historical or informational but is actively inspired by God Himself. It serves as a tool to teach, correct, and train us in living righteous lives. Engaging with Scripture as a conversation with God helps us grow and equips us to fulfill His purposes in our lives. This might sound daunting, but it's actually a profound gift. Through His Word, God reveals what is true and beautiful in us, as well as what needs to be healed or removed. This divine surgery is performed with precision and love, aiming to bring us into wholeness and alignment with God's will.

Romans 12:2 speaks to the transformative power of engaging with God's Word. As we meditate on Scripture and allow it to renew our minds, we become less influenced by worldly patterns and more attuned to God's will and purpose for our lives. This is the essence of being in a continual conversation with God through His Word.

We read Psalm 119:105 yesterday. It reminds us that the Word functions as a lamp to our feet and a light to our path. In a world where we are often faced with confusion and darkness, the truths of Scripture illuminate the way forward, offering clarity and hope. The decisions we face each day, from the mundane to the monumental, are informed and enlightened by the wisdom contained in God's Word.

Today, let us commit to engaging with the Scriptures not just as a routine or obligation, but as a vital conversation with the living God. Let's approach God's Word with openness and expectancy, ready to be challenged, encouraged, and transformed. As we read, meditate on, and apply the truths of Scripture, we'll find our lives increasingly aligned with God's heart and purposes.

Consider selecting a passage of Scripture to meditate on throughout the day. Ask God to speak to you through His Word, to illuminate areas of your life that need His touch, and to guide your decisions with His truth. As we do this, we'll discover that the Word of God is not only a source of wisdom and guidance but a wellspring of life-changing power.

Questions for Reflection and Intentional Transformation:

Transformation begins with the renewing of your mind. What practical steps can you take this week to regularly engage with Scripture, allowing it to shape your thoughts and actions?

As God's Word is 'God-breathed' and given for our benefit, what areas of your life do you feel you need more instruction, training, guidance or equipping?

How can you intentionally seek God's wisdom in these areas through His Word?

This is a time for intimate prayer. Have this conversation with your Heavenly Father, he's listening and ready to hear from you. After talking and sharing these things, give yourself time to just be still, to sit in his presence, be held in his comfort from being able to release that all to him. This is a time to be still in his presence and hear if he speaks. These steps can help you build intentional habits to help you better understand and live out God's perfect will.

Day 8: "Fostering a Spirit of Gratitude in All Circumstances"

Leading Scriptures:

- 1 Thessalonians 5:16-18 (NASB): "Rejoice always, pray without ceasing, in everything give thanks; for this is God's will for you in Christ Jesus."

- Psalm 34:1 (TPT): "Lord! I'm bursting with joy over what you've done for me! My lips are full of perpetual praise."

Gratitude is Intentional:

In the ebb and flow of life's seasons, maintaining a spirit of gratitude can sometimes feel like an overwhelming push out and sometimes an impossible challenge. Yet, the scriptures are clear: joy, prayer, and thanksgiving are not dependent on our circumstances but are a reflection of our relationship with God and our trust in His goodness.

1 Thessalonians 5:16-18 doesn't merely suggest gratitude as a good practice; it commands it as a way of life for those in Christ Jesus. This passage emphasizes a profound truth: gratitude is not a

feeling that comes and goes based on our situations but a choice to acknowledge God's presence and provision in every aspect of our lives.

Psalm 34:1 exemplifies this attitude of perpetual praise. The psalmist declares a resolve to burst with joy and continuously praise God, regardless of the circumstances. This expression of faith is not naivety; it's a deeply rooted acknowledgment of God's unchanging character and His faithfulness throughout all times.

Today, let us cultivate a heart of gratitude. Let's begin by reflecting on the blessings we often overlook—the gift of life, the beauty of creation, the love of family and friends, and above all, the unfailing love of God. As we shift our focus from our problems to God's provisions, our hearts will naturally overflow with thanksgiving.

Oftentimes we tend to focus on the issues of life. Sometimes we tend to focus on what we don't have. Many times we get so busy with living, working and life that we don't take time to acknowledge, rejoice and express gratitude. There is something powerful about intentional gratitude and praise. God is telling us to shift our thinking, reflect and acknowledge him and his faithfulness. Take a deep breath, hold it...Now let it out. That's his breath of life in you. There is so much we can express gratitude towards, even the senses we have and the functioning of the systems in our body. The many things we don't even see, like the ability to read and our minds. Thinking back and remembering intently the goodness in our life.

Practically, consider keeping a gratitude journal, listing at least three things you're thankful for each day. This simple practice can significantly shift our perspective, helping us to see God's hand in every detail of our lives.

As we embrace this posture of gratitude, we'll discover that the joy of the Lord truly is our strength, carrying us through every season of life with peace and purpose.

Questions for Reflection and Intentional Transformation:

What is one thing you can choose to be grateful for right now, no matter what circumstances lie ahead?

How does this intentional gratitude align with the call in 1 Thessalonians 5:16-18 to rejoice always and give thanks in everything?

Let's pray for the grace to rejoice always, to pray without ceasing, and to give thanks in everything.

Day 9: "Cultivating a Lifestyle of Worship"

Leading Scriptures:

- Romans 12:1 (NASB): "Therefore I urge you, brethren, by the mercies of God, to present your bodies a living and holy sacrifice, acceptable to God, which is your spiritual service of worship."

- Psalm 95:6-7 (TPT): "Come and kneel before this Creator-God; come and bow before the mighty God, our majestic maker! For we are the lovers he cares for and he is the God we worship. So drop everything else and listen to his voice!"

Worship is more than singing a song:

Worship is often associated with music or a service we attend, but the biblical view of worship encompasses so much more. It is a lifestyle, a way of living that honors God in every action, thought, and decision. Romans 12:1 invites us to see our lives as a continuous act of worship, presenting everything we are and do as an offering to God. This kind of worship goes beyond songs; it's about dedicating our daily lives to God's glory. In other words, every activity should be done in such a manner that God is honored and reverenced.

The call to worship in Psalm 95:6-7 is a call to recognize God's sovereignty and to respond with awe and humility. Worship, in this sense, is not just an individual act but a communal expression of reverence towards our Creator. It reminds us of our position in relation to God: He is the majestic maker, and we are the lovers He cares for. This understanding deepens our relationship with God, drawing us into a more intimate and reverent posture towards Him. The more you learn about God, fellowship with God and read his word, the more you will see him, how he fathers, his awesomeness and goodness. The more we know God and see him properly as our loving faithful father that loves us, won't withhold any good thing from us and has standards for his children because he wants the best for his children, the more our hearts will be filled with love from God and for God. As this grows in us, the more we have the confidence to praise him for WHO he is and share about him.

Cultivating a lifestyle of worship requires intentional practice. It's stepping into the truth that we were created to be holy, set apart, different and distinct from everything common in society. We were created for God's use, purpose, will and plan. It means waking up each day acknowledging God for who he is, his attributes and goodness, and thanking him for who he is and what he has done and is doing. It's deciding to dedicate that day to God and God's glory, whether in our work, relationships, or leisure. It involves recognizing God's presence in every moment and choosing to respond with gratitude, obedience, and praise.

Today, let's reflect on what it means to live as a holy and living sacrifice, acceptable to God. Let's ask God to help us see every moment as an opportunity to honor Him, see him and to transform our routines and activities into acts of worship that bring glory to him.

Questions for Reflection and Intentional Transformation:

How can we incorporate worship into the ordinary aspects of our daily lives?

How can we establish a personal intimate relationship with God and Christ that is infused with regular fellowship (friendly association and companionship), acknowledgement of his power, perfection and attributes and expressing these adorations and ascribing the highest regard?

As we go about our day, let's look for moments to express our love and reverence for God—whether that's through prayer, acts of kindness, or simply recognizing and acknowledging His goodness in the beauty of creation. Let's remind ourselves that every breath is a gift and every action can be an offering, as we live out a lifestyle of worship that pleases God and transforms our world.

Day 10: "Fostering Unity in the Body of Christ"

Leading Scriptures:

- Ephesians 4:2-6 (NASB): 'with all humility and gentleness, with patience, showing tolerance for one another in love, being diligent to preserve the unity of the Spirit in the bond of peace. There is one body and one Spirit, just as also you were called in one hope of your calling; one Lord, one faith, one baptism, '

- 1 Corinthians 12:27 (TPT): "You are the body of the Anointed One, and each of you is a unique and vital part of it."

You are an essential part to the unity within the body:

Unity within the body of Christ is not merely a nice idea; it's a vital aspect of our faith. The scriptures call us to actively pursue and maintain unity, recognizing that we are all part of something much larger than ourselves. As members of Christ's body, each of us has a unique role to play, and our individual contributions are essential to the health and function of the whole.

Ephesians 4:3 challenges us to be diligent in preserving unity, highlighting that it requires effort and intentionality. Unity doesn't mean uniformity or the absence of diversity; rather, it's the harmonious working together of different parts for a common purpose. This unity is maintained through the bond of peace, a shared commitment to love, forgiveness, reconciliation, and mutual respect.

1 Corinthians 12:27 reminds us of our identity as the body of Christ. Just as a body relies on the function of each part, so too does the body of Christ depend on each member. Our diversity is our strength, allowing us to meet a wider range of needs and reach different people. When we appreciate and support the unique gifts and callings of our brothers and sisters in Christ, we strengthen the entire body.

Today, let's reflect on our role in fostering unity within our faith communities. Let's pray for God's guidance in creating a culture of unity and peace, asking Him to reveal ways we can contribute to the health and vitality of His body.

As we go about our day, let's commit to being agents of unity, choosing words and actions that build up rather than tear down. Let's celebrate the diversity within the body of Christ, recognizing that every member has something valuable to contribute. We can do this by Intentionally acknowledging what we see, complimenting others on the value they contribute and appreciating them for their virtues. Sharing these mirrors encourages, lets others feel seen and helps them see themselves. In doing so, we not only strengthen our spiritual family but also offer a compelling witness to the world of the love and harmony that can be found in Christ, in the royal family, God's Kingdom.

Questions for Reflection and Intentional Transformation:

Are there areas where we can be more supportive or open to the contributions of others?

Are there brothers or sisters that you can intentionally compliment and show more love towards, in your kindness and patience?

Let's look for opportunities to do just that. Ask God to show you and lead you in embracing humility to see each other properly and showing more love to foster unity in the body. That also means being patient and cordial with others as they grow, mature and heal. It definitely means being patient with God as he works in and through others in their growth, healing and transformation. Love is Kind and Patient. God is Love. They will know us by our Love.

Rest Stop: Preparing for the next Leg of the Journey.
From Exploring & Reflecting →Considering God's Word &
Practicing It

We have just completed 10 days of intentional reflection in God's Word and reflecting on our lives, personally. We are ⅓ of the way through this 30-Day Personal Journey. Day 10 takes us beyond ourselves and focuses our attention to the vital role we have in the unity of the body. The Body with so many different diverse parts, all blessed with unique gifts, abilities and functions within the Body. The Body of Christ, The Body of Believers, the Royal Family... All believers are on the same path, yet at different places dealing with different experiences that have impacted their souls. We are all on the journey of life. We are seeking God ,insight, wisdom and direction for our journey and purpose. We are renewing our minds on our personal journey and growing spiritually, one day at a time.

Now that we have cultivated a rhythm of reflecting on God's Word and way, while thinking about what we've been thinking, our past experiences and how we've been living and considering God's Word anew, We are stepping into transformation. We are transforming from the inside out. It starts in the heart and in our minds. Now, we can actively practice what we are learning about our Heavenly Father, to intentionally consider his words and ways in regards to what we do, and how we live it out.

As we continue to learn, fellowship and talk to God and Christ more, we can ask his Holy Spirit to help us do what may at times, feels weird or goes against what we've always thought and done. We are intentionally taking in his word, thinking about it, and putting it into action. As we do this, we grow in alignment with how our Heavenly Father sees, his ways and what he wills for his children. We are looking at ourselves, renewing our mind with God's truth and perspective, then actively practicing the values and ways of our Heavenly Father.

We are growing in the light of God's Kingdom, embracing the Culture of the Kingdom. The Kingdom Culture is very different from the culture of this society. It's about Love, Learning, Community, Joy, Peace and Unity, in Purpose and on Purpose, all for his glory. It's about eternal Life and Living "THE LIFE" with God as our Faithful Heavenly Father and Jesus as Big Brother, Lord and King, connected and led by his Holy Spirit. We are called to learn the King, See the Father , be in relationship, fellowship, practice righteousness, represent them as a royal son or daughter, heir to God the Father and Co-heir with Christ the King. We are blessed with the help and guidance of the Holy Spirit within us. We are the Royal Family, chosen Kings and Queens, learning the royal standards and ways, embracing the culture, living out our royalty intentionally. We are learning about our Creator and being renewed in his likeness and image. We are following the example and ways of the King, empowered by the Holy Spirit within, as our guide, teacher and comforter. We are embracing our personal journey, we are taking our place. We are learning and transforming, day by day, from the inside out.

In Christ we are new. We are called to have fellowship with Christ. Now, let's embrace the renewing of our mind and the transformation for a New Life and Lifestyle, a lifestyle of gratitude & worship. A lifestyle of regular fellowship and growing in relationship with Yahweh, our Heavenly Father and Creator, and with Christ, Our Brother, Lord and King through the Holy Spirit.

This is an opportunity to talk with God about this. Express the desire to grow in your worship and closeness, for an open heart to embrace the journey of transforming you from the inside out, for a new Life and

Lifestyle. We are embracing the transformation into a new lifestyle that fellowships, delights, honors, praises and worships God. An inner transformation in you that renews your mind and cultivates the values, virtues and culture of God's Royal Family, the Kingdom of God.

As we continue this 30-day journey and begin Day 11, we'll meditate on God's Word and seek ways to apply it throughout our day. This is a move from knowledge to understanding, from reflection to intentional practice. We are called to be doers of the Word, not just hearers. As children of the Most High, we're created with a purpose, uniquely designed to be transformed into the likeness of Christ.

We are intentionally taking time and making room to know our Father God, His Word and Truths and our King more deeply. This is a call to grow in fellowship, to transform intentionally, and to practice what we learn with each step. Transformation is a process that is intentional. Living with purpose, we embrace God's values, growing and thriving spiritually as we journey into the culture and community of God's Family, The Kingdom of Light. *Moving forward in our journey,* we will practice what we learn through ***Practical Application.***

Day 11: "The Joy of Giving in God's Kingdom"

Leading Scriptures:

- 2 Corinthians 9:7 (NASB): "Each one must do just as he has purposed in his heart, not grudgingly or under compulsion, for God loves a cheerful giver."

- Acts 20:35 (TPT): 'I've left you an example of how you should serve and take care of those who are weak. For we must always cherish the words of our Lord Jesus, who taught, 'Giving brings a far greater blessing than receiving."

Giving is how we love, serve and take care of the family:

In the economy of God's Kingdom, the principles often seem upside down to the world's ways. One such principle is the joy and blessing found in giving. The world tells us to accumulate, protect, and prioritize our own needs, but God invites us into the beautiful paradox of generosity—where giving not only blesses others but also enriches our own lives.

2 Corinthians 9:7 emphasizes the attitude with which we give. Our giving should not be out of obligation or pressure but from a place of joy and purposeful decision in our hearts. God cherishes the cheerful giver, not because He needs our gifts, but because He knows the transformative power of generosity in our lives. When we give freely, we align ourselves with God's generous nature, opening our hearts to receive and experience His abundance in new ways.

Acts 20:35 underscores the blessing inherent in giving. The words of Jesus, "It is more blessed to give than to receive," turns our worldly understanding on its head. This teaching invites us to look beyond our immediate desires and consider the deeper joy found in service and generosity. When we give—whether of our resources, time, or talents—we participate in God's work of care and provision for His people. God works in us and through us for each other.

Today, let's consider how we might embody the spirit of generosity in our lives. We can be generous and give money to others, yet generosity goes beyond money. Sometimes a thoughtful gift given blesses you and the other person. It's about giving to others. There are so many things that we can give to others that money can not buy. We can give a smile, a hello, a kind word, a compliment, a hug, a "thinking of you" text or a conversation that shows interest and concern. What gifts and talents were you blessed with? We can share our gifts and talents to help and serve others.

One of the precious priceless things in life that we can share is time. Time is precious and non refundable. Time is the unit of life. Time is our currency of life. We measure life with time. As we practice generosity, we'll find that it not only changes the lives of those we give to but transforms our own hearts, drawing us closer to the heart of God, who is the ultimate Giver.

Questions and Reflections → Intentional Practice

What resources, talents, or time do we have that we could share to bless others?

Reflect on the blessings you have received through giving in the past.

How did those experiences impact your relationship with God and with others?

Let's ask God to show us opportunities to give and to help us do so with a cheerful heart, expecting nothing in return.

Practical Application: **Intentional Practice**

Today, let's be intentional about giving today. Decide in your heart what you will give freely and joyfully. Let today be a day that you intentionally give to others. Start small if you like. Maybe today can be a day of giving sincere compliments throughout your day or a day to give your time and attention to others by calling to check on others.

Day 12: "Fostering Gratitude in Everyday Life"

Leading Scriptures:

- 1 Thessalonians 5:18 (NASB): "In everything give thanks; for this is God's will for you in Christ Jesus."

- Colossians 3:16 (TPT): 'Let the word of Christ live in you richly, flooding you with all wisdom. Apply the Scriptures as you teach and instruct one another with the Psalms, and with festive praises, and with prophetic songs given to you spontaneously by the Spirit, so sing to God with all your hearts!'

Cultivating Gratitude is Intentional:

Cultivating a heart of gratitude is not merely an exercise in positive thinking; it is an essential practice for spiritual growth and well-being. The Scriptures remind us that giving thanks in all circumstances is not only a command but a pathway to experiencing God's presence and peace in our lives. It shifts our focus from what we lack to the abundance we have in Christ.

1 Thessalonians 5:18 encourages us to give thanks in everything. This isn't to say we should be thankful for evil or hardship itself, but within every situation, we can find reasons to thank God. Whether it's His presence, His strength, the lessons learned, or the growth experienced, there's always a silver lining that reflects His goodness.

Colossians 3:16 speaks to letting the teachings of Christ dwell in us richly, resulting in wisdom and gratitude. This gratitude is expressed in our worship of acknowledging God for who he is and who he has been, our interactions with others, and our internal dialogue. It's a holistic approach that acknowledges God's hand in every aspect of our lives. It's intentionally thinking of things that are good, true and praise worthy.

Gratitude is a powerful choice that transforms our perspective, bringing us closer to God and grounding us in His goodness. In 1 Thessalonians 5:18, we're reminded that giving thanks in every circumstance is part of God's will for us, inviting us to trust His provision and sovereignty, even when life feels uncertain. This practice of gratitude is a way of seeing life through a Kingdom lens, where we recognize God's hand at work in both the blessings and challenges we encounter. Colossians 3:16 encourages us to let Christ's teachings fill our hearts, leading us to respond with gratitude through psalms, hymns, and spiritual songs. By intentionally choosing gratitude, we create space for God's peace and wisdom to flood our lives, helping us to grow spiritually and to encourage others along the way. Gratitude becomes not just a response but a lifestyle, enabling us to live each day with a heart full of worship and thanksgiving.

By consciously practicing gratitude, we train our hearts to recognize God's goodness in every situation, fostering a deeper sense of joy and contentment in our journey with Him.

Practical Application & Today's Challenge:

Today, let's intentionally practice gratitude. Start the morning by listing three things you're thankful for. They can be as simple as the sunshine, a good night's sleep, or the availability of food and water. Throughout the day, make it a point to recognize and appreciate small blessings you might usually overlook.

Here's a simple challenge: Reach out to someone who has made a difference in your life and express your appreciation. It could be a family member, friend, teacher, mentor or colleague. Let them know specifically what you're thankful for and how they've impacted you.

In the evening, reflect on your day and identify moments where you saw God's hand at work. It could be in a conversation, a moment of peace, an unexpected resolution to a problem, or simply the beauty in nature. End your day with a prayer of thanks, acknowledging God's faithfulness and the many ways He blesses you.

Day 13: "The Strength Found in Godly Community"

Leading Scriptures:

- Hebrews 10:24-25 (NASB): "And let us consider how to encourage one another in love and good deeds, not abandoning our own meeting together, as is the habit of some, but encouraging one another; and all the more as you see the day drawing near."

- Hebrews 10:24-25 (TPT):'Discover creative ways to encourage others and to motivate them toward acts of compassion, doing beautiful works as expressions of love. This is not the time to pull away and neglect meeting together, as some have formed the habit of doing. In fact, we should come together even more frequently, eager to encourage and urge each other onward as we anticipate that day dawning.'

- Ecclesiastes 4:9-10 (NASB): "Two are better than one because they have a good return for their labor. For if either of them falls, the one will lift up his companion. But woe to the one who falls when there is not another to lift him up."

Community is Essential to Our Growth and Maturity:

In the Kingdom of God, as God's Royal Family, in our faith walk journey, the value of community cannot be overstated. We were not designed to navigate the complexities of life in isolation. The Scriptures highlight the strength, encouragement, and accountability that come from being part of a godly community. This divine principle of fellowship is foundational to our growth and perseverance in faith. We are the body. We are better together.

Hebrews 10:24-25 emphasizes the importance of gathering together to spur one another on toward love and good deeds. This mutual encouragement is especially crucial as we anticipate the return of Christ. It's in the context of community that we find strength to face challenges, comfort in times of sorrow, and joy in shared victories. It is in community that we heal, receive mirrors to see ourselves properly, rekindle joy, grow and mature in life giving relationships, and have new experiences that provide a counter from old past traumatic experiences. Community is not a neighborhood. Community is a garden of shared values, connectedness, social bonds, new family, encouragement, resources, safety and support.

Ecclesiastes 4:9-10 offers a simple yet profound truth: life is better together. The support system found in a godly community is invaluable. Whether we're on the mountaintop or in the valley, having someone to share the journey with makes all the difference. It's about lifting each other up, bearing one another's burdens, and walking together in faith.It's about having safe spaces to talk, share, ask questions, learn more, confess one to another and intercede for one another. God did not intend for us to do life alone.

Practical Application & Today's Challenge:

Engage with your faith community more deeply today. If you're part of a small group or Bible study, take a moment to reach out to a member you haven't spoken to recently. Offer a word of encouragement, ask how you can pray for them, or simply check in to see how they're doing.

Here's today's challenge: If you're not currently active in a community, consider taking a step towards finding one. This could be through your local church, an online Christian forum, or a local small group or Bible study group. Remember, the goal is not just to receive support but to give it as well. There is someone needing what you have to share about your experiences, insight, lessons and wisdom gained along the way in your life's journey.

Reflect on your experiences within Christian fellowship. How has being part of a community impacted your faith journey? Write down a few thoughts or share them with a friend. As we invest in the lives of others, we not only fulfill God's command but also discover the joy and strength that come from walking in unity with our brothers and sisters in Christ.

Day 14: "The Transformative Power of Forgiveness"

Leading Scriptures:

- Ephesians 4:31-32 (NASB): "Let all bitterness, wrath, anger, clamor, and slander be put away from you, along with all malice. Be kind to one another, tender-hearted, forgiving each other, just as God in Christ also has forgiven you."
- Matthew 18:21-22 (TPT): "'Later Peter approached Jesus and said, "How many times do I have to forgive my fellow believer who keeps offending me? Seven times?" Jesus answered, "Not seven times, Peter, but seventy times seven times!"

Forgiveness is Essential in God's Family and a Kingdom Virtue:

Forgiveness is one of the most powerful and challenging principles within the Christian faith. It demands a letting go of past hurts and offenses, not as an act of weakness but as one of strength and obedience to God. The scriptures for today invite us into a lifestyle of forgiveness, mirroring the boundless mercy God has shown us through Christ. Jesus' sacrifice and forgiveness are inseparable. Jesus shared this truth, If we forgive others, God will forgive us. If we do not forgive others, God will not forgive us.

Ephesians 4:31-32 calls for a radical transformation of our hearts and relationships. It's a call to replace bitterness and anger with kindness and compassion. This process begins with forgiveness, not as a one-time event but as a continuous choice to release others from the debt of their wrongs against us, just as God has done for us in Christ.

Matthew 18:21-22 stretches our understanding of forgiveness even further. Jesus' response to Peter's question about the limits of forgiveness is not just about keeping count but about eradicating the concept of limits when it comes to forgiveness. This teaching challenges us to the core, especially when the wounds are deep and the pain feels insurmountable.

Forgiveness is not just a spiritual command; it's a transformative force that liberates both the forgiver and the forgiven. When we choose to forgive, we release the burden of bitterness and resentment that weighs down our hearts and minds. Ephesians 4:31-32 reminds us that harboring anger and malice impacts our spirit, distancing us from the peace and joy that God desires for us. By choosing to be tender-hearted and forgiving, we reflect God's grace, which softens the hardness within us and restores broken relationships. This act of forgiveness is essential not only for our emotional well-being but also for the health of the body of Christ. When we let go of offenses and extend mercy, we promote unity and healing within the community, allowing God's love to flourish among us.

God is Love. Love is kind and patient. Offense comes from a lack of understanding. There are many people who are functioning from brokenness and hurting hearts. Sometimes past hurt and brokenness has been there so long, they are not even aware that they have done something or said something that was hurtful, harmful and unloving. This is where love is key. Being kind, cordial and patient with others and God.

It's about seeing them with an understanding that the behavior is not the person. It's an understanding that hurt people hurt people whether they realize it or not. With an openness to this understanding, it's easier to see a person and not just their behavior. To love is to be kind and patient. We are called to be patient with others and with God. We are all on a journey in life. We are at different developmental places and maturity levels. We are called to be patient with God as he works in, through and on the hearts of others. This is so we don't take personal offense and so we can forgive one another.

In Matthew 18:21-22, Jesus' command to forgive "seventy times seven" speaks to the limitless nature of forgiveness, urging us to break the cycle of grudges and hostility. Every act of forgiveness brings healing, not only to our souls but to our relationships and the larger body of Christ. Holding onto offenses creates division, but forgiveness mends, allowing us to experience the fullness of God's Kingdom on earth.

Through the transformative power of forgiveness, we are set free, walking in the freedom Christ purchased for us, fostering peace, love, and unity in all our interactions.

This is also true when it comes to forgiving yourself. We are called to Love others AS we love ourselves. Embrace forgiveness, for others and for yourself.

Practical Application:

Today, take a moment to reflect on any areas of unforgiveness in your heart. Is there someone you need to forgive? It could be a family member, friend, colleague, or even yourself. Consider writing a letter of forgiveness to them. You don't necessarily have to send it, but the act of writing it can be a powerful step towards releasing the burden of unforgiveness.

Here's today's challenge: Take time to think of who you have not forgiven. Pray for the strength to forgive, asking God to help you forgive and see the person(s) who hurt you through His eyes. Remember, forgiveness does not mean forgetting the offense or condoning the behavior; it means choosing to release the hold it has on your heart.

Forgiveness is a journey, and it might not happen overnight. However, each step towards forgiveness is a step towards freedom, peace, and a closer walk with God. Ask God to help you forgive and release any grudges. As we choose to forgive, we open ourselves up to the healing and transformative work of the Holy Spirit in our lives. Forgiveness opens the path for God to flow. Unforgiveness restricts and hinders the flow of God in us. Forgive to Flow!

Day 15: "The Discipline of Prayer: Connecting with God Daily"

Leading Scriptures:

- 1 Thessalonians 5:16-18 (NASB): "Rejoice always, pray without ceasing, in everything give thanks; for this is God's will for you in Christ Jesus."

- Luke 11:1-2 (TPT): "'One day, as Jesus was in prayer, one of his disciples came over to him as he finished and said, "Would you teach us a model prayer that we can pray, just as John did for his disciples?" So Jesus taught them this prayer: "Our heavenly Father, may the glory of your name be the center on which our life turns. May your Holy Spirit come upon us and cleanse us. Manifest your kingdom on earth.

- Luke 11:2 (NASB): 'And He said to them, "When you pray, say: ' Father, hallowed be Your name. Your kingdom come.'

Prayer is a Lifestyle of Personal Fellowship, not a duty or a hit or miss activity:

Prayer is the lifeline of our faith, a direct line to the heart of God. It's not just about asking for things but about cultivating regular fellowship to grow in relationship with the Creator of the universe. The scriptures for today highlight the importance and power of maintaining a consistent prayer life.

1 Thessalonians 5:16-18 encourages us to rejoice always, pray without ceasing, and give thanks in all circumstances. This trio of commands might seem difficult, but they're interconnected. Rejoicing and thanksgiving set the tone for our prayer life, creating a posture of gratitude and joy that permeates our communication with God. Praying without ceasing doesn't mean we're in a constant state of sitting in prayer but that we're always in a posture of readiness and connection with God, keeping the lines of communication open throughout our day. Prayer is Fellowship throughout our day.

Luke 11:1-2 shows us that even the disciples needed guidance on how to pray. Jesus' response, teaching them what we now call "The Lord's Prayer," provides a template for our prayers. It begins with worship ("Father, hallowed be your name"), aligns us with God's purposes ("your kingdom come"), and then moves into our needs and concerns. This model prayer underscores the importance of prioritizing God's will and kingdom in our prayers before focusing on our personal requests.

Prayer is more than a ritual or a moment of need; it is an ongoing, intentional communion with God that strengthens our spirit and deepens our relationship with Him. In 1 Thessalonians 5:16-18, we are encouraged to pray without ceasing, keeping a continual connection with God that influences every part of our day. This discipline of constant prayer is not about formality or routine but about aligning our hearts with God's presence, fostering a lifestyle that rejoices in His goodness and seeks His guidance in all circumstances. Prayer becomes a way of inviting God into every detail of our lives, keeping us anchored in His peace and grounded in His will.

When Jesus taught His disciples to pray in Luke 11:1-2, He gave them a model that centered on God's holiness and His Kingdom purposes. This teaching reminds us that prayer is an invitation to participate in God's work on earth, asking Him to manifest His Kingdom in and through us. As we practice this daily discipline, we begin to see prayer as a vital exchange, where our desires, fears, and hopes are met by God's wisdom, peace, and guidance. In approaching prayer this way, it becomes a lifestyle of fellowship that transforms us from within and aligns us more closely with God's heart, empowering us to live each day as vessels of His Kingdom.

Practical Application:

Today, let's practice the discipline of prayer by setting aside specific times to pray intentionally. Begin your day with a prayer of thanks and a request for God's presence to lead you and ask his Holy Spirit to guide you. Throughout the day, take short breaks to reconnect with God, perhaps using a verse or a part of "The Lord's Prayer"as a prompt. Or just share and talk.

Here's today's challenge: Try to integrate prayer into your daily activities. For example, while doing household chores, commuting, or during breaks at work, use these moments to lift up silent prayers. These don't have to be long or eloquently spoken; they just need to be heartfelt.

End your day with a reflective prayer. Look back over the day, thank God for His blessings and presence, and lift up any concerns or needs. Ask for peace and rest as you prepare to end the day.

As we make prayer a priority and regular part of our daily routine, we'll find ourselves more attuned to God's voice and presence in our lives. This discipline of prayer strengthens our faith, brings clarity to our calling, and deepens our relationship with our heavenly Father.

Day 16: "Living a Life of Humility"

Leading Scriptures:

- Philippians 2:3-4 (NASB): "Do nothing from selfishness or empty conceit, but with humility of mind regard one another as more important than yourselves; do not merely look out for your own personal interests, but also for the interests of others."
- 1 Peter 5:5 (TPT):'In the same way, the younger ones should willingly support the leadership of the elders. In every relationship, each of you must wrap around yourself the apron of a humble servant. Because: God resists you when you are proud but multiplies grace and favor when you are humble. '

Humility is a value in God's Family and Virtue within the Kingdom Culture:

Humility is a virtue that's often misunderstood and undervalued in our culture, yet it's central to the Christian faith, God's Royal family and Kingdom culture. Humility is essential for a life that truly reflects Jesus. Philippians 2:3-4 challenges us to adopt a mindset that's radically counter-cultural: to consider others as more significant than ourselves and look out for their interests in addition to our own.

This kind of humility is not about thinking less of ourselves but thinking of ourselves less, shifting our focus to how we can serve and uplift those around us.

1 Peter 5:5 reminds us of the grace that comes with humility. God's economy is one where the humble are exalted, not by their own efforts, but by the hand of God who gives grace and favor to the humble. This scripture also emphasizes the importance of mutual submission and respect within the community of believers, regardless of age or status.

Living a life of humility means embracing a servant's heart, one that seeks to uplift others and honor God above all. In 1 Peter 5:5, we're reminded to "wrap around yourself the apron of a humble servant," highlighting that humility is an active, intentional choice. It's not about diminishing our own value but about seeing others through God's eyes, with love and compassion. Humility invites us to let go of pride and self-centeredness, making room for God's grace to work powerfully in our lives. When we choose humility, we position ourselves to receive His favor, as God promises to "multiply grace and favor" for the humble.

True humility is the pathway to unity, peace, and strength in our relationships, both within God's family and in the world. As Philippians 2:3-4 teaches, when we place others' needs alongside or even before our own, we begin to reflect the heart of Jesus, who came not to be served but to serve. Living with humility allows God to shine through us, helping us to build a Kingdom culture of honor, love, and selflessness that reveals His character to the world.

Practical Application:

Today, seek out opportunities to live out humility in your interactions and decisions. Start with prayer, asking God to give you a heart of humility and to reveal areas where pride may be hindering your relationships with Him and others.

Here's today's challenge: Identify one practical way you can place someone else's interests above your own. It might be as simple as letting someone else choose where to eat, letting someone go in front of you, actively listening when someone shares their thoughts without immediately offering your own or offering your time to help someone with a task.

Consider also how you can submit to and honor the authority figures God has placed in your life, whether that's within your family, church, workplace, or community. Reflect on how you can support and encourage them in their responsibilities.

End your day by reflecting on the experiences where you practiced humility. How did it impact your relationships and your own heart? Humility isn't a one-time act but a lifestyle choice that deeply transforms us, our relationships and our communities.

Day 17: "Seeking God's Wisdom in Decision Making"

Leading Scriptures:

- James 1:5-6 (NASB): "But if any of you lacks wisdom, let him ask of God, who gives to all generously and without reproach, and it will be given to him. 'But he must ask in faith without any doubting, for the one who doubts is like the surf of the sea, driven and tossed by the wind. '

- "Proverbs 3:5-6 (TPT): "Trust in the Lord completely, and do not rely on your own opinions. With all your heart rely on him to guide you, and he will lead you in every decision you make. Become intimate with him in whatever you do, and he will lead you wherever you go."

Seeking God's Guidance - Trusting His Wisdom for Every Decision Cultivates Our Kingdom Culture:

In a world filled with choices and crossroads, the quest for wisdom remains paramount. Wisdom is not merely about accumulating knowledge but about understanding how to apply that knowledge in ways that align with God's will. James 1:5 offers an incredible promise: God is not only willing but eager to grant us wisdom generously, without finding fault.

This assurance underscores the character of God as a loving Father, ready to guide His children through the complexities of life. God did not intend for us to live life without divine guidance.

Proverbs 3:5-6 presents a formula for divine guidance that involves complete trust in the Lord, an admonition to not lean on our own understanding, and the instruction to acknowledge Him in all our ways. This scripture highlights the importance of seeking God's will in our decisions, promising that He will direct our paths when we do.

Seeking God's wisdom is essential to navigating life's decisions with clarity, confidence, and peace. Proverbs 3:5-6 reminds us to trust in the Lord wholeheartedly, releasing our reliance on personal understanding and opinions. This dependence isn't a sign of weakness but of strength, as it anchors us in God's perfect perspective and understanding, which surpasses our limited view. When we invite God into our decision-making process, we align our hearts with His will and open ourselves to His direction, allowing Him to lead us "in every decision" we make.

James 1:5-6 reinforces this invitation by urging us to seek wisdom from God with faith and expectancy, free from doubt. God's promise to give wisdom generously and without reproach speaks to His loving nature; He desires to guide us, not only in major life choices but also in daily decisions. Approaching Him for wisdom in faith strengthens our relationship with Him and builds our trust in His ability to provide the best guidance for our lives. This kind of wisdom keeps us steady, unmoved by the shifting tides of circumstance, enabling us to walk confidently in His path.

Practical Application:

Today, identify a decision you're currently facing. It could be something significant or relatively minor. Begin by praying for wisdom, specifically asking God to help you see the situation from His perspective and to provide clear guidance on the path to take.

Here's today's challenge: Spend some time in the Word. Look for scriptures that speak to your situation or provide general guidance about godly wisdom and decision-making. Google it. Reflect on how these scriptures might apply to your decision. Give yourself time and space for stillness, calm and quietness.

Intentionally embrace quietness. You can walk in nature or find a solitude space where you can be still and silent. Jesus often withdrew to pray and hear from God. Remember, as King of God's Kingdom, he is our example to follow.

Then, seek godly counsel. Reach out to a trusted Christian friend, mentor, or leader who can provide insight and perspective. Share your thoughts and concerns, and be open to the advice they offer, weighing it against the truth of God's Word.

Finally, take some time to be still before God, listening for His voice. Sometimes, God's guidance comes through a gentle nudge, a sense of peace, or the alignment of circumstances. Be patient and remain open to His leading, even if it requires waiting for clarity.

End your day by journaling your thoughts and any insights you've received. Record the steps you're taking to seek God's wisdom and any confirmations or directions you feel He has provided. Remember, seeking God's wisdom in decision-making is an act of faith and submission to His sovereign will, trusting that He knows what's best for us and is faithful to guide us in His perfect timing.

Day 18: "The Blessing of Serving Others"

Leading Scriptures:

- Matthew 20:26-28 (NASB): "It is not this way among you, but whoever wishes to become great among you shall be your servant, and whoever wishes to be first among you shall be your slave; just as the Son of Man did not come to be served, but to serve, and to give His life a ransom for many."

- Galatians 5:13 (TPT): 'Beloved ones, God has called us to live a life of freedom. But don't view this wonderful freedom as an excuse to set up a base of operations in the natural realm. Constantly love each other and be committed to serve one another.'

Embracing Greatness Through Serving Others:

In a world that often equates greatness with power, wealth, or status, Jesus presents a radical redefinition: true greatness is found in servanthood. Matthew 20:26-28 reminds us that the path to greatness in the Kingdom of God is not about ascending the ladders of human success but about descending into the humility of service, following the example of Jesus Himself, who came not to be served but to serve.

Galatians 5:13 connects this servanthood with the freedom we have in Christ. Freedom means that we become so completely free of self-indulgence that we become servants of one another, expressing love in all we do. This freedom is not for self-indulgence but for selfless love and service to one another. It's a freedom from the bondage of selfish desires, enabling us to live out love in practical acts of service. This kind of service is not born out of obligation but out of the overflow of Christ's love within us.

Serving others is one of the most profound expressions of Christ's love, a call to embody His heart in our everyday lives. When Jesus redefined greatness as servanthood in Matthew 20:26-28, He showed us that true fulfillment comes not from seeking status but from pouring out our lives for the benefit of others. Serving isn't about gaining recognition; it's about reflecting Jesus, who humbly served and gave Himself as a ransom for many. In this, we find a powerful example that aligns us with Kingdom values, where each act of service becomes a testament to God's love and grace. We were created to be an answer to a problem. We serve by being a solution.

Galatians 5:13 reminds us that the freedom we've received in Christ isn't for self-centered living but for self-giving love. True freedom allows us to step beyond our own desires, leading us to serve others in a spirit of generosity and compassion. Is there any passion in you towards helping others or solving a problem in our world? When we serve from this place of love, our actions become more than just good deeds; they become part of our worship and a practical extension of God's Kingdom on earth. This kind of service blesses both the giver and receiver, fostering a culture of humility, love, and unity that reflects the heart of God's Kingdom.

True greatness in God's Kingdom is found in serving others with humility and love, reflecting Christ's example of selfless service. Through the freedom we have in Christ, we are called to step beyond self-interest and express His love in practical ways, becoming solutions to the needs around us. Serving others transforms our actions into worship and extends God's Kingdom on earth, creating a culture of compassion, unity, and grace.

Practical Application:

Today, seek ways to serve those around you. Start small and local. Look for opportunities in your home, workplace, or community. It could be as simple as doing a chore typically done by someone else, offering to help a coworker with a project, or volunteering a few hours of your time for a local charity or church event.

Here's today's challenge: Reflect on the motives behind your acts of service. Are they to gain recognition or out of genuine love and compassion? Ask God to purify your motives and to fill you with His selfless love.

Take a moment at the end of the day to journal about your experiences. How did serving others make you feel? Did you notice any shift in your relationships or in your own heart? Reflecting on these questions can deepen your understanding of true greatness as defined by Jesus and encourage you to continue walking in the blessing of serving others.

Day 19: "The Power of Prayer in Personal Transformation"

Leading Scriptures:

- James 5:16 (NASB): "Therefore, confess your sins to one another, and pray for one another so that you may be healed. The effective prayer of a righteous man can accomplish much."
- Colossians 4:2 (TPT): "Be faithful to pray as intercessors who are fully alert and giving thanks to God."

Embrace Prayer as a Transformative Kingdom Lifestyle:

Prayer is a fundamental aspect of the Christian life, it's the foundation of living as God's chosen Children, it's a Kingdom Lifestyle of God's Royal Family. Prayer is a powerful means through which we communicate with God, express our desires, and intercede for others. It's also a transformative practice that shapes us, drawing us closer to God and aligning our hearts with His will. James 5:16 highlights the healing and powerful outcomes of prayer, not just in the physical sense but in spiritual and emotional healing as well. It underscores the importance of community and mutual support in our journey of faith.

Colossians 4:2 encourages us to be devoted to prayer, staying vigilant and thankful. This persistence in prayer is not a passive activity but an active engagement with God, where we are both speaking and listening. It's in this place of prayerful attentiveness that we find the strength to face life's challenges and the wisdom to make godly decisions.

Prayer is the lifeblood of our spiritual growth, a powerful practice that shapes and transforms us into the likeness of Christ. Through prayer, we experience a deep connection with God, allowing His presence to mold our thoughts, heal our hearts, and align our desires with His purposes. James 5:16 emphasizes the importance of praying within the community of believers, showing us that mutual confession and intercession bring profound healing and restoration. This kind of prayer builds bonds within God's Royal Family, reminding us that we are not alone in our journey and that our prayers for one another hold the power to bring about real change.

In Colossians 4:2, we're called to be faithful and alert in our prayer life, approaching God with gratitude and an open heart. This intentional devotion to prayer keeps us grounded, heightening our awareness of His guidance and giving us strength to navigate life's challenges. As we persist in prayer, both individually and within our community, we allow God's transformative work to take root in our lives, creating a foundation of trust, resilience, and purpose. In this way, prayer becomes the catalyst for personal transformation, empowering us to live out our Kingdom identity with clarity and conviction, rooted in an unwavering relationship with God.

Prayer is a transformative practice that connects us deeply with God, aligns our hearts with His will, and fosters healing and growth within His Kingdom community. Through faithful and intentional prayer, we gain strength, wisdom, insight, direction and purpose, empowering us to live out our Kingdom identity with belief and grace.

Practical Application:

Today, dedicate a specific time for prayer, focusing on personal transformation and intercession for others. Start by confessing any known sins to God, asking for His forgiveness and cleansing. This act of confession not only brings healing but also deepens your intimacy with God.

Here's today's challenge: Turn your attention outward and pray for the needs of others. It could be for a friend facing a difficult situation, a family member in need of guidance, or even broader issues affecting your community or the world. Remember, your prayers are powerful and effective.

As you pray, also take time to listen. Take time to be still in quietness. Prayer is a two-way conversation. Ask God to speak to you, to reveal his wisdom, to reveal areas in your life that He wants to transform, and to guide you in His will.

Finally, express your gratitude to God. Thank Him for His presence, His provision, and His unfailing love. Gratitude shifts our focus from our problems to God's greatness and faithfulness. Keep a journal of your prayers and any insights or answers you receive. This practice can be a powerful reminder of God's work in your life and through your prayers.

Rest Stop: Preparing for the Last Leg of the Journey

From Reflecting, Considering & Practicing
→ Taking Intentional Actions to Practice & Build Habits

We have just completed 19 days of intentional reflection on God's Word and practicing doing what we have learned from the word, in our lives. We are ⅔ of the way through this 30-Day Personal Journey Guide.

During this journey, we have cultivated a rhythm of reading and reflecting on God's Word and his ways, while thinking about how we can actually put those values and virtues into daily living and engaging with others. We have increased our communication and time of fellowship with God while learning essential aspects of living as God's Royal family to cultivate a Kingdom Mindset and Lifestyle. We have explored and tried different practical ways of applying God's Word to practice living out Kingdom virtues through daily experiences. We've been considering God's Word anew and being intentional about doing what we are learning. We are renewing our minds and transforming from the inside out.

Day 20 will take us beyond exploring and practicing what we are learning to intentionally taking action to build regular practices in our daily lives. We will intentionally embrace God's Word and Values by living what we learn. We will grow and develop a Kingdom mindset. We will build habits that will intentionally transform our mind and life. We will embrace the journey of living a Kingdom Lifestyle as chosen, beloved, Children of The Most High God. We will grow in our fellowship and relationships, knowledge, understanding and divine wisdom.

We will Embrace God's Royal Family values and cultivate the Kingdom of God Culture while experiencing the abundant life in our personal journey. We are growing in relationship with the Most High and Our Appointed King, Jesus Christ, while walking with his Spirit as our guide and teacher through life. We are on a journey of transformation and faithfulness within our lifelong personal journey. As we pursue and journey with Yahweh, Our Heavenly Father, and Jesus Christ, Our King, we will continue to grow spiritually in truth, belief, wisdom and faith, empowered to live as God's Children, His Royal Family, The Kingdom of God.

Day 20: "Deepening Our Connection with God Through Prayer"

Leading Scriptures:

- 1 Thessalonians 5:16-18 (NASB): "Rejoice always, pray without ceasing, in everything give thanks; for this is God's will for you in Christ Jesus."

- James 5:16 (TPT): "Confess and acknowledge how you have offended one another and then pray for one another to be instantly healed, for tremendous power is released through the passionate, heartfelt prayer of a godly believer."

Heartfelt prayer deepens our bond with God and strengthens unity in the Kingdom community:

Prayer serves as the heartbeat of our spiritual life, a dynamic conversation that fosters a deep, personal relationship with the Divine. Unlike a monologue, prayer is a dialogue, a sacred exchange where we speak to God and, importantly, listen for His response. It encompasses praise, thanksgiving, confession, and petition, reflecting the multifaceted nature of our relationship with our Creator.

1 Thessalonians 5:16-18 challenges us to live in a state of constant communication with God, integrating prayer into every aspect of our lives. This continual prayer doesn't mean we are in a non-stop, verbal conversation with God but that we maintain a constant awareness of His presence to communicate with God. This can transform mundane moments into opportunities for spiritual growth and reflection. Whether we're experiencing joy, navigating challenges, or simply going about our daily tasks, every situation presents a chance to connect with God.

James 5:16 underscores the transformative power of prayer, not just for the individual but within the community. Confession and intercessory prayer—praying on behalf of others—bring healing and unleash God's power. This mutual vulnerability and support demonstrate the strength of God's people united in prayer, affirming the collective faith that activates the miraculous.

Prayer deepens our connection with God by fostering an ongoing, intimate relationship that brings transformation, healing, and guidance. When we embrace the call in 1 Thessalonians 5:16-18 to "pray without ceasing," we develop an awareness of God's constant presence, allowing every moment—whether joyful or challenging—to become an opportunity to commune with Him. This unbroken connection not only strengthens our faith but also aligns our heart with His, keeping us grounded in gratitude and reliant on His guidance. Delight yourself in God. Just ask and believe to receive his grace and wisdom.

James 5:16 emphasizes the power of communal prayer and the vulnerability that confession brings. When we share our struggles, acknowledge our offenses, and pray for one another, we open the door to God's healing power. This practice of intercessory prayer builds unity and unleashes God's miraculous power, reinforcing that prayer is not just a private discipline but a gift that strengthens the entire body of Christ. In this way, prayer becomes a channel for God's grace, deepening our personal relationship with Him and building a foundation of trust and love within the community.

Additionally, try to cultivate a practice of "listening" during your prayers. After you've shared your heart with God, spend some time in silence, allowing God's spirit to speak to you. This might be through the Scriptures, an inner prompting, peace in your decision-making, or an encouragement that comes to mind.

Practical Application →To Build Life Giving Habits:

To weave prayer more deeply into the fabric of our daily life, consider adopting the following practices:

- Morning Offering: Begin each day by offering it to God, asking Him to guide your thoughts, words, and actions.
- Prayer Alarms: Set several alarms throughout the day as reminders to pause and pray. These moments can be brief but are powerful pauses to realign your focus on God.
- Prayer Walks: Turn regular walks into prayerful reflections, using the time to pray for your community, your loved ones, and for God's creation that surrounds you.
- Evening Reflection: End your day with a prayerful review of the day's thoughts, actions and events, acknowledging God's presence in all things and seeking His wisdom, guidance, protection & peace for any unresolved issues.

By integrating these practices into our daily routine, we foster a more profound, ongoing connection with God. Prayer becomes less about fulfilling a religious duty and more about nurturing a life-giving relationship. As we open our hearts to God regularly,, we become more attuned to His voice and guidance, experiencing the richness of a life lived in continuous fellowship with Him. This is the abundant life of access.

Day 21: "Experiencing God's Love and Extending It to Others"

Leading Scriptures:

- 1 John 4:16 (NASB): "We have come to know and have believed the love which God has for us. God is love, and the one who abides in love abides in God, and God abides in him."
- John 13:34-35 (TPT): "So I give you now a new commandment: Love each other just as much as I have loved you. For when you demonstrate the same love I have for you by loving one another, everyone will know that you're my true followers."

God's Love must be received, recognized and accepted to experience and extended:

Understanding and accepting God's love is foundational to our identity as Children of God, Followers of Jesus, citizens of God's Kingdom. It's from this deep well of divine knowledge and love that we see God properly, see ourselves as God does and love ourselves. This renewed perspective of love without being sexually connected, helps us learn what love is through a new lens and gain strength and wisdom in learning how to love ourselves and others properly. The journey of faith is, at its core, a journey of love—learning to recognize, receive and accept God's love and then reflecting it back to ourselves and out into the world.

1 John 4:16 emphasizes that knowing and believing in God's love is essential for our relationship with Him. To abide in God and have Him abide in us is to live within the sphere of His love, letting it fill and transform every part of our lives. This love is not based on our performance or worthiness but is a gift of grace, available to all who believe.

John 13:34-35 challenges us to live out this love in our relationships. Jesus sets the standard, commanding us to love others as He has loved us. This sacrificial, unconditional love is the mark of true discipleship. It's through this love that the world experiences, sees and knows Jesus.

Living in the fullness of God's love empowers us to reflect His heart to others. 1 John 4:16 assures us that abiding in God's love is foundational to our relationship with Him. When we allow His love to permeate our lives, it transforms us, enabling us to see ourselves and others through His compassionate perspective. This reminds us that to abide in God's love is to remain securely rooted in His unchanging character, trusting that His love is not earned but freely given. When we truly understand and believe in this love, it reshapes our hearts and minds, enabling us to extend the same grace and compassion to others as well to ourselves. This love is a gift of grace, freely given and not dependent on our actions, which fills us with a sense of worth and security that flows out to those around us.

God calls us to demonstrate this love in our relationships, modeling the selfless, sacrificial love of Jesus. This love becomes our testimony, revealing God's heart to the world and identifying us as His true followers. Through such love, being kind and patient with others and God, we become vessels of God's Kingdom, inviting others to experience His presence and goodness.

Practical Application →Choose Intentional Actions to Build Life Giving Habits:

- Reflect on God's Love: Spend time meditating on scriptures that speak of God's love for you. Ask God to help you grasp the width, length, height, and depth of His love. To recognize, receive and accept his love. To notice and embrace how God loves us and uses others to share his love so we can experience true love. (Ephesians 3:14 -19).

- Act of Love: Choose one tangible act of love you can perform today. It could be something as simple as sending an encouraging message, helping a neighbor, or making time for someone who needs to talk.
- Prayer for Love: Pray for the ability to see others as God sees them and to love them accordingly. Ask for opportunities to demonstrate His love in practical ways.
- Love Journal: Consider starting a journal to record your experiences of giving and receiving love. Note any changes in your relationships or personal growth as you focus more on loving others.

As we intentionally focus on recognizing, accepting, receiving, experiencing and extending God's love, we'll find our own lives enriched and our relationships deepened. This journey of love is not always easy, but it is the path through which we truly come to know God, receive his love, begin to truly see and love ourselves and make Him known to others by his love. Through our love, the world can see a glimpse of the divine, his love, likeness and image, drawing others closer to the heart of God. As we embrace this love and extend it, we become true reflections of Christ, and our lives testify to His presence and our transformation, showing the world what it means to be His disciples and what it is to love.

Day 22: "The Power of God's Peace in Overcoming Anxiety"

Leading Scriptures:

- Philippians 4:6-7 (NASB): "Be anxious for nothing, but in everything by prayer and supplication with thanksgiving let your requests be made known to God. And the peace of God, which surpasses all comprehension, will guard your hearts and your minds in Christ Jesus."
- 1 Peter 5:7 (TPT): "Pour out all your worries and stress upon him and leave them there, for he always tenderly cares for you."

Experience Peace Beyond Understanding Through Pouring and Trusting in God:

Anxiety can often feel like a constant companion in our fast-paced, uncertain world. It creeps into our lives, stealing our peace and joy. Yet, the Word of God offers us a profound antidote to anxiety: the peace of God. This peace is not merely the absence of trouble but a deep, abiding sense of security and calm that comes from trusting God's Word, his wisdom, instructions, sovereignty, his supreme power, and love.

Philippians 4:6-7 instructs us not to be anxious about anything but instead to bring everything to God in prayer. This directive is both a command and a promise. When we lay our concerns before God, acknowledging our need for Him, He promises to guard our hearts and minds with His peace. This peace is not something the world can give or take away; it's a gift from God that transcends our understanding and circumstances.

1 Peter 5:7 encourages us to cast all our anxieties on God because He cares for us. This scripture is a beautiful reminder of God's personal love and concern for each of us. He invites us to release our burdens to Him, not because He is unaware of them, but because He desires to carry them for us.

God's peace is a powerful, unwavering force that meets us in the midst of life's storms, providing security and calm that go beyond our understanding. Philippians 4:6-7 reassures us that **when** we bring our anxieties to God with gratitude, He responds by guarding our hearts and minds with His supernatural peace. This isn't a peace that fades with circumstances, but a divine assurance that anchors us, reminding us of His presence and sovereignty over every detail of our lives.

1 Peter 5:7 further encourages us to surrender our worries to God, emphasizing His tender care for each of us. God doesn't merely tolerate our struggles; He lovingly invites us to place our burdens on Him and leave it there, knowing He is strong enough to carry them. By trusting Him with our anxieties, we open our hearts to experience a peace that flows from His love, transforming our fears into confidence and our worries into worship. In doing so, we find true rest and strength in His presence. We rest in GODfidence and peace. (GODfidence is confidence in God, not ourselves... what I like to describe as trusting in his sovereignty, wisdom, leading and power to handle it, his faithfulness in providing and guiding us along the way)

Practical Application → Choose Intentional Actions to Build Life Giving Habits:

- Prayer of Release: Take a moment to write down the things that are causing you anxiety. Then, pray over each item, physically releasing them to God. Imagine placing each worry into His hands.
- Thanksgiving Reminder: Create a daily habit of listing three things you're thankful for. Gratitude shifts our focus from our problems to God's provisions.
- Peaceful Meditations: Spend a few minutes each day meditating on verses about God's peace. Consider memorizing Philippians 4:6-7 or 1 Peter 5:7 to remind yourself of God's promises when anxiety arises. Speak them out loud, remind yourself of truth, What God has already said concerning you and his way.
- Community Support: Share your struggles with a trusted friend or prayer partner. Allow them to pray with you and for you, offering the support of a godly community.

As we practice these steps, remember that God's peace depends not on our circumstances but on His unchanging nature. Trusting Him and casting our cares on Him brings peace, knowing we are securely held by our loving Father. This builds GODfidence.

Day 23: "Cultivating Patience in a World of Instant Gratification"

Leading Scriptures:

- James 1:4 (NASB): "And let endurance have its perfect result, so that you may be perfect and complete, lacking in nothing."
- Colossians 3:12 (TPT): "You are always and dearly loved by God! So robe yourself with virtues of God, since you have been divinely chosen to be holy. Be merciful as you endeavor to understand others, and be compassionate, showing kindness toward all. Be gentle and humble, unoffendable in your patience with others."

Embrace Patience in a Fast-Paced World:

In our modern time of living, where the pace of life seems to accelerate daily and the expectation for immediate results grows ever stronger, the virtue of patience can feel both counterintuitive and increasingly necessary. Patience—a fruit of the Spirit—is essential for deepening our faith and fostering meaningful relationships, allowing us to endure trials and trust in God's timing.

James 1:4 speaks to the transformative power of patience, or endurance, in our spiritual journey. This spiritual journey is one that will war against your faith and test your faith. Your faith is your complete trust and confidence in God. It is through the testing of our faith that patience is developed, leading us toward spiritual maturity and completeness. This process of refinement, though often challenging, equips us to navigate life's difficulties with God's grace and resilience.

Colossians 3:12 reminds us that we are deeply loved by God and calls us to clothe ourselves with compassion, kindness, humility, and patience. This directive emphasizes the relational aspect of patience, highlighting its role in understanding and forgiving others. In practicing patience, we reflect God's character to the world, embodying His love and grace in our interactions.

In a culture driven by instant results, cultivating patience is a countercultural act of faith that aligns us with God's purpose and timing. James 1:4 encourages us to let endurance complete its work in us, leading us to spiritual maturity and a deeper sense of wholeness. This patience isn't passive but an active, trusting perseverance that prepares us to handle life's challenges with resilience and peace.

Colossians 3:12 reminds us that, as God's dearly loved children, we are called to embody virtues like compassion, kindness, and humility, all of which require patience. By practicing patience with others, we reflect God's unending grace and love. Patience allows us to see people through God's eyes, forgiving their faults and showing them understanding and compassion. In doing so, we foster deeper, more meaningful relationships and demonstrate a Kingdom lifestyle that is patient with God and values God's timing over instant gratification.

Practical Application → Choose Intentional Actions to Build Life Giving Habits:

- Practicing Patience Daily: Identify a situation in your daily routine that typically tests your patience. Make a conscious decision to approach this situation with calmness and grace, asking God to help you see it as an opportunity to grow in patience.

- Patience Journal: Start a patience journal. Note instances where you struggled with patience and reflect on what triggered your impatience. Also, record the moments you successfully practiced patience and how it made a difference in the outcome or your emotional state.
- Study Patience in Scripture: Spend some time each week studying biblical characters who exemplified patience and what we can learn from their experiences. Consider Abraham's long wait for a son, Joseph's endurance through trials, or Jesus' patience with His disciples.
- Community Challenge: Engage with friends, family, or your small group about the topic of patience. Share your struggles and successes, and pray for one another to grow in this area.

As we intentionally cultivate patience in our lives, we'll not only experience personal growth but also contribute to a more loving, understanding, and grace-filled world. Let us lean into God's strength and wisdom, trusting that He is at work in us, developing the fruit of the Spirit in us, perfecting us through every season of waiting, through every test of faith and patience.

Day 24: "Finding Strength in Weakness"

Leading Scriptures:

- 2 Corinthians 12:9-10 (TPT) 'But he answered me, "My grace is always more than enough for you, and my power finds its full expression through your weakness." So I will celebrate my weaknesses, for when I'm weak I sense more deeply the mighty power of Christ living in me. So I'm not defeated by my weakness, but delighted! For when I feel my weakness and endure mistreatment—when I'm surrounded with troubles on every side and face persecution because of my love for Christ—I am made yet stronger. For my weakness becomes a portal to God's power.'
- Isaiah 40:29 (NASB): "'He gives strength to the weary, And to him who lacks might He increases power. '

Embracing God's Strength in Our Weakness:

In a culture that often celebrates self-sufficiency, independence and strength, admitting to weakness can feel like a failure. However, the Kingdom of God operates on principles that turn worldly wisdom on its head. The Scriptures offer us a paradoxical, contrasting truth: our weaknesses, rather than disqualifying us, can become the channel for God's power, strength and grace to flow in us and through us.

2 Corinthians 12:9-10 reveals Paul's radical perspective on weakness. After pleading with the Lord to remove his "thorn in the flesh," Paul receives a life-changing revelation. God's grace is not only sufficient in our weakness, but it is precisely in our inability that His strength is made perfect. This divine strength enables us to endure trials and challenges not with resentful reluctant acceptance, but with joy, knowing that in our vulnerability, the power of Christ is magnified.

Isaiah 40:29 offers further encouragement, reminding us that God provides strength to the weary and increases the power of the weak. This verse speaks to all who have felt overwhelmed or inadequate, assuring us that God's provision of strength is not dependent on our natural abilities but on His limitless resources.

In God's Kingdom, our weakness is not a limitation but an opportunity for His power to shine through us. 2

Corinthians 12:9-10 teaches us that God's grace is most evident when we embrace our limitations, allowing His strength to work in our lives. Paul's experience reveals a profound truth: when we acknowledge our need for God, we open ourselves to His power, transforming our weaknesses into sources of strength. This shift allows us to approach challenges not with despair but with confidence, knowing that Christ's power rests upon us.

Isaiah 40:29 further reassures us that God renews and strengthens those who feel weak or weary. This promise reminds us that we don't have to rely on our own strength alone. Instead, we can lean into God's limitless energy and find rest in His support. Through our dependence on Him, we find that true strength is not found in self-sufficiency but in surrendering to the One who never tires or grows weary.

Practical Application → Choose Intentional Actions to Build Life Giving Habits:

- Identify and Embrace Weakness: Take time to reflect on the areas of your life where you feel weakest. Instead of hiding or lamenting these, bring them before God in prayer, asking Him to demonstrate His power in these areas.

- Testimony of Weakness: Consider sharing your experience of finding strength in weakness with a trusted friend or small group. Your story can encourage others to see their own vulnerabilities through the lens of God's grace.
- Strength in Scripture: Memorize 2 Corinthians 12:9-10 or Isaiah 40:29 as a personal reminder of God's promise to be your strength in times of weakness.
- Acts of Trust: Challenge yourself to step out in faith in an area where you feel inadequate, trusting that God will provide the strength you need. It could be a small act of service, a difficult conversation, or a new opportunity you've been hesitant to pursue.

By embracing our weaknesses and relying on God's strength, we not only experience His power in profound ways but also bear witness to His grace and sufficiency. In the kingdom of God, admitting weakness is the first step to accessing divine strength and grace, transforming our challenges into opportunities for growth and testimony.

Day 25: "The Freedom Found in God's Forgiveness"

Leading Scriptures:

- Psalm 32:1-2 (NASB): "How blessed is he whose transgression is forgiven, whose sin is covered! How blessed is the man to whom the Lord does not impute iniquity, And in whose spirit there is no deceit!"
- 1 John 1:9 (TPT): "But if we freely admit our sins when his light uncovers them, he will be faithful to forgive us every time. God is just to forgive us our sins because of Christ, and he will continue to cleanse us from all unrighteousness."

Embracing Freedom Through God's Forgiveness:

The weight of guilt and shame from our past mistakes can often feel like a heavy chain, limiting our freedom and joy. Yet, the gospel brings us the incredible news of God's forgiveness, offering us a liberation that transcends human understanding. Through Christ's sacrifice, we are invited into a life marked not by our failures but by the boundless grace of God.

Psalm 32:1-2 highlights the profound joy and blessing of receiving God's forgiveness. The imagery of sin being covered and iniquity not being counted against us reveals the depth of God's mercy. It's a mercy that allows us to live in freedom and peace, knowing our past does not define us, and our mistakes are not beyond the reach of God's redeeming love.

1 John 1:9 reassures us of the faithfulness of God to forgive. This forgiveness is not conditional on our ability to make amends or earn God's grace but is freely given when we confess our sins. It's in this confession and acknowledgment of our need for God that we find continual cleansing and the strength to move forward in righteousness.

God's forgiveness offers a freedom that lifts the weight of guilt and shame, allowing us to walk in joy and peace. Psalm 32:1-2 reveals the blessing of forgiveness, illustrating that when God covers our sins, we are released from the burden of past mistakes. This covering is an act of divine mercy that empowers us to live confidently, knowing that we are no longer defined by our failures but by God's redeeming love.

1 John 1:9 emphasizes that God's forgiveness is assured whenever we come to Him in honesty and

humility. Our sins are cleansed, not by our merit, but through Christ's sacrifice. This ongoing forgiveness invites us to approach God openly, embracing a freedom that renews our hearts and strengthens our walk in His righteousness. In God's forgiveness, we find true freedom and a fresh start each day.

God's forgiveness brings freedom from guilt and shame, allowing us to live in peace and joy. Through Christ's sacrifice, we are cleansed and empowered to walk in righteousness, defined not by our past but by God's boundless grace.

Practical Application → Choose Intentional Actions to Build Life Giving Habits:

- Confession as a Path to Freedom: Set aside time for quiet reflection and prayer, asking God to reveal any areas of sin or unresolved guilt in your life. Approach Him with a humble and contrite heart, confessing your sins and accepting His forgiveness.

- Reflect on God's Forgiveness: Meditate on the truths of Psalm 32:1-2 and 1 John 1:9. Consider writing them down or creating a visual reminder of God's forgiveness to look back on when feelings of guilt or shame arise.
- Forgiveness Journal: Start a forgiveness journal. Document instances where you experienced God's forgiveness, noting how it impacted your sense of freedom and peace. This can serve as a powerful testimony of God's grace in your life.
- Share the Gift of Forgiveness: If you feel led, share your experience of finding freedom in God's forgiveness with someone who may be struggling with guilt or shame. Your testimony could be a beacon of hope, pointing them towards the transformative power of God's grace.

Embracing the freedom found in God's forgiveness allows us to shed the chains of our past and step into the light of His grace. It's a journey from darkness into marvelous light, where we are continually renewed and empowered to live a life of purpose and joy.

Day 26: "Embracing God's Call to Rest"

Leading Scriptures:

- Matthew 11:28-30 (TPT): "Are you weary, carrying a heavy burden? Come to me. I will refresh your life, for I am your oasis. Simply join your life with mine. Learn my ways and you'll discover that I'm gentle, humble, easy to please. You will find refreshment and rest in me. For all that I require of you will be pleasant and easy to bear."
- Exodus 20:8-10 (NASB): "Remember the sabbath day, to keep it holy. Six days you shall labor and do all your work, but the seventh day is a sabbath of the Lord your God; in it you shall not do any work, you or your son or your daughter, your male or your female servant or your cattle or your sojourner who stays with you. '

Regular Rest is Essential for Our Journey:

In today's fast-paced world, the concept of rest often gets lost amidst the hustle of daily life. Yet, the Scriptures remind us that rest is not only a divine gift but also a command. It's an invitation from God not just to cease from physical labor but to find spiritual renewal and peace in Him. Jesus shared that "The Sabbath was made for man, and not man for the Sabbath". Our bodies were not designed to always work long hours and stay busy throughout each day. Matthew 11:28-30 offers a profound invitation from Jesus to all who feel overwhelmed by life's burdens. This rest is more than physical relaxation; it's a deep, soul-level rest that comes from walking in relationship with Jesus. His yoke is not a burden but a means of learning His gentle, humble way of life that brings peace to our souls.

Exodus 20:8-10 points to the Sabbath as a holy, set-apart time for rest and worship. This commandment is not merely about physically stopping from work but about dedicating time to remember, worship, and rest in the presence of God. It serves as a weekly reminder of God's provision and sovereignty, encouraging us to trust Him with our time and our work. It's a time to rest in God's rest.

God's call to rest is a gracious reminder that we are not defined by busyness or constant productivity, but by our relationship with Him. Rest is a divine gift, inviting us to pause, recharge, and reconnect with God's presence. In Matthew 11:28-30, Jesus extends a gentle invitation to all who are weary, promising rest that goes beyond physical relief to reach the depths of our souls. His yoke is light and His way gentle, teaching us that true rest is found in Him, as we release our burdens and learn to walk at His pace.

Exodus 20:8-10 underscores this invitation with the command to observe the Sabbath, setting aside dedicated time each week to rest and remember God's provision. Sabbath rest is a reminder of our dependence on Him, allowing us to step back from the demands of daily life and realign our hearts with His truths, peace and purpose. By embracing God's call to rest, we affirm that our value lies not in our accomplishments but in our relationship with Him, as beloved Children and members of His Kingdom.

Practical Application → Choose Intentional Actions to Build Life Giving Habits:

- Create Space for Rest: Identify a specific time this week to unplug from your regular activities and work. Use this time for restful activities that rejuvenate your spirit and soul, such as spending time in nature, reading, praying, or practicing a hobby that brings you joy.

- Sabbath Practice: Consider how you can incorporate a Sabbath rest into your weekly routine. This doesn't necessarily mean doing nothing; it's about making intentional choices to rest in God's presence and enjoy the life He's given you.
- Rest in Prayer: Spend some time in prayer, casting your burdens and worries onto Jesus. Ask for His peace and rest to fill your soul. Reflect on the areas of your life where you struggle to trust God and ask for the grace to surrender these to Him.
- Journal Reflection: Write down your experiences of rest and any insights you gain during this time. Reflect on how taking deliberate time to rest affects your relationship with God and your overall well-being.

By intentionally embracing God's call to rest, we acknowledge our human limitations and our need for God's renewing presence. Rest, as God designed it, is an act of faith and trust in Him who sustains all things, reminding us that our worth is not tied to our productivity but to our identity as beloved children of God.

Day 27: "The Call to Live Righteously"

Leading Scriptures:

- 1 Peter 1:15-16 (NASB): "But like the Holy One who called you, be holy yourselves also in all your behavior; because it is written, 'YOU SHALL BE HOLY, FOR I AM HOLY.'"
- Titus 2:11-12 (TPT): "For God's marvelous grace has manifested in person, bringing salvation for everyone. This same grace teaches us how to live each day as we turn our backs on ungodliness and indulgent lifestyles, and it equips us to live self-controlled, upright, and godly lives in this present age."

Choosing Righteousness in a World of Compromise:

The call to live a righteous life is a foundational aspect of our faith and identity as Children of God, but it is also a journey marked by grace, growth, and transformation. Holiness, as described in the Scriptures, is not merely about adhering to a set of rules; it's about reflecting the character of God in our lives, a process that is both personal and communal, affecting every aspect of our behavior and interactions.

1 Peter 1:15-16 reminds us that holiness is not optional but integral to our identity as Children of God,

followers of Christ. To be holy, as God is holy, means to set ourselves apart from sin and the patterns of this world. It's a divine invitation to live lives that are distinct, not for the sake of religion but as a tribute, honor and respect to the One who called us.

Titus 2:11-12 highlights the role of grace in our pursuit of righteousness. Grace is not just the unmerited favor that saves us; it's also the power that transforms us. This grace empowers us to decern and not engage in ungodliness and worldly passions. It empowers us to live self-controlled, upright, and virtuous lives. The Kingdom life is one of constant learning and growing, being guided by the Holy Spirit and given grace that empowers us. This is the same grace that first brought us to God, his gift.

Living righteously is a counter-cultural act that stands in stark contrast to the norms of a world often shaped by self-indulgence, moral compromise, and shifting standards. 1 Peter 1:15-16 calls us to a life of holiness, setting us apart from patterns of behavior that the world might celebrate, like unrestrained ambition, exploitation, or perverse lifestyles that disregard God's design for purity and integrity. Holiness means choosing to reflect God's nature, rejecting what is popular when it conflicts with what is true and pure according to His Word.

Titus 2:11-12 reveals that grace empowers us to live differently. This grace empowers us to decline and diminish engaging in ungodliness and worldly passions, which might include practicing dishonesty, promiscuity, drunkenness, and materialism that are often promoted in the world around us. God's grace transforms us, inviting us to pursue self-control, godliness, and integrity over indulgence or cultural trends. By living in this way, we honor God and become witnesses to a Kingdom culture that values truth, purity, and righteousness above the temporary pleasures and perversions of the world.

Practical Application → Choose Intentional Actions to Build Life Giving Habits:

- **Evaluate Your Influences:** Regularly assess the messages, media, and relationships that influence your thoughts and actions. If something consistently encourages self-indulgence, moral compromise, or distracts you from God's standards, consider reducing or replacing it with influences that foster spiritual growth. Fill your mind with God's Word, sermons, worship, and teachings that align with a Kingdom mindset (Romans 12:2).
- **Daily Decisions for Righteousness:** Make a conscious effort to choose righteousness in your daily decisions. This could mean speaking

words of life instead of negativity, choosing forgiveness over bitterness, or setting boundaries to protect your heart and mind from ungodly influences.

- **Intentionally Choose Holiness:** Holiness is built on choices. Whether in conversation, workplace ethics, entertainment, or personal thoughts, choose what aligns with God's values, even if it's counter to cultural norms. Over time, these small choices to pursue integrity, purity, and kindness will create a pattern of righteousness that reflects God's character in your life (Philippians 4:8).

- **Community and Accountability:** Surround yourself with believers who also seek to live righteously. Consider forming or joining a small group, prayer circle, or mentorship relationship with fellow believers where you can share your struggles and victories, encourage one another and pray for one another regularly and have fun doing life with each other righteously.

As we pursue righteousness, let us remember that it's a journey marked by grace. We will stumble, but God's grace is sufficient to pick us up, teach us, and lead us forward. Living a righteous life is not about achieving perfection but about growing closer to God and fostering a lifestyle of holiness, helping you reflect God's character, love and holiness in our world, in a culture often opposed to it.

Day 28: "The Gift of Godly Wisdom"

Leading Scriptures:

- James 1:5 (NASB): "But if any of you lacks wisdom, let him ask of God, who gives to all generously and without reproach, and it will be given to him."
- Proverbs 2:6-8 (TPT): "'Wisdom is a gift from a generous God, and every word he speaks is full of revelation and becomes a fountain of understanding within you. For the Lord has a hidden storehouse of wisdom made accessible to his godly ones. He becomes your personal bodyguard as you follow his ways, protecting and guarding you as you choose what is right."

Pursuing and Receiving the Gift of Godly Wisdom:

In our journey of faith and life, we often face decisions that require more than just human intellect or experience. The need for divine wisdom becomes apparent as we navigate complex situations and relationships. Godly wisdom is a precious gift, one that God promises to give generously to those who seek it.

James 1:5 reassures us that God is not only willing but eager to provide us with wisdom. This wisdom is not dispensed sparingly or with conditions but is given freely to all who ask in faith. Unlike human wisdom, which can be flawed and limited, God's wisdom encompasses divine insight, moral integrity, and the ability to discern the best course of action in every situation.

Proverbs 2:6-7 paints a beautiful picture of wisdom as a treasure from God, full of revelation and understanding. This passage highlights that wisdom is more than just practical advice; it's a foundational attribute of a righteous life, providing protection and guidance to those who value integrity.

Godly wisdom is a profound gift, offering guidance and protection beyond what human understanding alone can provide. James 1:5 encourages us to seek this wisdom with confidence, knowing that God generously provides it to anyone who asks in faith. His wisdom brings clarity and discernment, enabling us to make decisions that align with His purpose and goodness.

Proverbs 2:6-8 reveals that wisdom is a hidden treasure from God, accessible to those who walk in righteousness. This wisdom becomes a source of divine insight, acting as a "fountain of understanding" and even a "personal bodyguard" for those who choose to live by God's ways. With His wisdom, we gain more than direction; we gain a steady foundation, fortified by God's truth and safeguarded by His presence.

Godly wisdom is a priceless gift, offered generously to those who seek it, providing divine guidance, protection, and clarity. By aligning with God's wisdom, we gain insight and strength to make choices that reflect His purpose and truth in our lives.

Practical Application → Choose Intentional Actions to Build Life Giving Habits:

- **Daily Prayer for Wisdom**: Begin each day by asking God for wisdom in decisions, interactions, and challenges. Trust that He will provide insight generously as you seek His guidance (James 1:5)

- **Reflect on Scripture for Guidance**: Regularly meditate on verses that reveal God's perspective, like Proverbs 2:6-8. Reflecting on God's Word cultivates discernment and aligns your choices with His values, becoming a source of daily guidance.

- **Seek Wise Counsel**: Surround yourself with spiritually mature individuals who prioritize God's wisdom. Engage in discussions, ask for advice, and allow their insights to help you grow in discernment and integrity (Proverbs 11:14).

- **Pause Before Decisions**: Practice pausing and praying before making significant choices. Allowing time to listen for God's direction deepens reliance on His wisdom, promoting thoughtful, godly responses over impulsive actions.

These practices will help you continually draw from God's wisdom, building a Kingdom-focused mindset and lifestyle.

As we actively seek God's wisdom, let us do so with the assurance that He desires to grant it to us abundantly. This divine wisdom not only equips us to make sound decisions but also draws us closer to the heart of God, where true understanding and revelation are found. By valuing and applying godly wisdom, we navigate life's challenges with grace and discernment, reflecting God's character in our choices and actions.

Day 29: "Embracing God's Timing in Our Lives"

Leading Scriptures:

- Ecclesiastes 3:1 (NASB): "There is an appointed time for everything. And there is a time for every event under heaven—"
- Habakkuk 2:3 (NASB): "For the vision is yet for the appointed time; it hurries toward the goal and it will not fail. Though it delays, wait for it; for it will certainly come, it will not delay long."

Trusting the Perfect Rhythm of God's Timing:

In the swift currents of our modern life, where the pace of change accelerates and the pressure to achieve grows, the divine principle of God's timing remains a steadfast beacon of hope and guidance. Our journey with God often involves seasons of waiting, times of resting, intervals of being sat down unexpectedly to restore and periods that challenge our patience and stretch our faith. Yet, these moments are not without purpose. They are divinely orchestrated opportunities for growth, reflection, and preparation.

Ecclesiastes 3:1 introduces a profound and comforting truth: there is a divine timing for everything. This passage invites us to trust in God's sovereignty over our lives, recognizing that He orchestrates our days and seasons with wisdom and purpose. It's a call to surrender our agendas and trust that God's timing is perfect, even when it doesn't align with our expectations.

Habakkuk 2:3 speaks directly to the heart wrestling with the tension of divine promises and their fulfillment. The vision—God's promises and plans for our lives—has its appointed time. Though its arrival may seem delayed by our human standards, it is assuredly on its way, hastening toward its fulfillment. This verse encourages us to steadfastly hold onto hope, affirming that God is not bound by our timelines and that His plans for us will not tarry beyond their divine appointment.

Embracing God's timing invites us to rest in His wisdom, trusting that every season in our lives has purpose. Ecclesiastes 3:1 reminds us that there is an appointed time for everything, a comforting assurance that God has planned each chapter of our journey with divine precision. This truth challenges us to surrender our timelines and trust that God's timing is perfect, even when it diverges from our own plans.

Habakkuk 2:3 speaks to the tension of waiting for God's promises. While we may grow impatient or discouraged, this verse reassures us that God's plans are set and will arrive at just the right moment. Waiting is not a passive season but an active one, full of growth, preparation, and trust. By embracing God's timing, we find peace in knowing that He is faithful to fulfill every vision and promise in our lives, exactly when He knows it is best.

Practical Application → Choose Intentional Actions to Build Life Giving Habits:

- **Practice Patience in Small Decisions**: Start with everyday situations, choosing patience over urgency. Whether waiting in line or for a response, these moments build a habit of trusting God's timing and preparing our hearts for bigger seasons of waiting.

- **Biblical Characters Study**: Choose a biblical character who experienced a significant period of waiting (e.g., Joseph, Abraham, Sarah, David) and study their story. Note how God used the waiting period to shape their character and fulfill His promises in ways that far exceeded their expectations.

- **Prayer for Patience, Trust and Contentment:** Begin each day by asking God for patience and a stronger trust in His perfect timing. Pray for wisdom to understand the actions you need to take and for peace in waiting on His guidance for all else. In moments of impatience, ask for His calming presence and the grace to rest in His plan, letting go of any urge to rush or control outcomes, trusting that each delay holds a purpose in His design.

- **Create a Vision Board:** Make a vision board that represents God's promises and the dreams He's placed in your heart. Use it as a visual reminder to pray and trust in God's timing, especially when doubts and impatience arise.
- **Find Purpose in Waiting**: Use seasons of waiting for growth and preparation, learning new skills, deepening spiritual practices, or serving others. Embracing these times as active seasons of refinement aligns us with God's Kingdom purposes for our lives.

As we learn to embrace God's timing, we discover the peace that comes from surrendering to His will and the joy of seeing His promises unfold in our lives. Let us hold fast to the assurance that while we wait, God is actively at work, weaving the tapestry of our lives into a masterpiece that reflects His glory and goodness.

Day 30: "Stepping Forward in Faith - A Journey of Continuous Growth"

Leading Scriptures:

- Philippians 3:13-14 (NASB): "Brethren, I do not regard myself as having laid hold of it yet; but one thing I do: forgetting what lies behind and reaching forward to what lies ahead, I press on toward the goal for the prize of the upward call of God in Christ Jesus."
- Joshua 1:9 (TPT): 'I repeat, be strong and brave! Do not yield to fear nor be discouraged, for I am Yahweh your God, and I will be with you wherever you go!'

Passionately Pursue and Press Onward in Faith and Transformation:

As we conclude our 30-day journey of spiritual reflection and growth, it's important to recognize that our walk with God is a continuous journey. Each day has presented us with truths and practices to deepen our relationship with God, align ourselves with His kingdom values, and live out our faith in tangible ways. We've explored themes of trust, love, humility, service, prayer, and many others, each forming a vital part of our foundation in Christ.

Philippians 3:13-14 encourages us to keep moving forward in our spiritual journey, pressing on toward the goal of the upward call of God. This passage reminds us that spiritual growth is a lifelong process, where we continually seek to know Christ more deeply and to live in a way that reflects His love and truth.

Joshua 1:9 offers divine assurance of God's presence and strength as we step into the future. It's a call to courage and faith, knowing that wherever our path leads, we do not walk alone. God is with us, empowering us to overcome fear and discouragement.

Stepping forward in faith is a commitment to ongoing growth, a journey where each step draws us closer to God's purpose. Philippians 3:13-14 inspires us to leave past mistakes and successes behind, focusing instead on the upward call of growing in Christ, our divine identity and   This journey isn't about reaching perfection overnight; it's a process of continual transformation, one where we align our lives more closely with God's love, truth, and grace each day.

Joshua 1:9 reassures us that as we face the unknown, God's presence goes with us, calling us to courage and strength. Walking in faith means moving beyond fear and into trust, knowing that God empowers us to press forward. With Him as our guide, we are equipped to navigate life's challenges, confident that every step we take is under His watchful care and part of His plan for our lives. We are growing in GODfidence as we embrace our personal journey, pursue God passionately, learn his values and live them out intentionally by faith.

Practical Application → Choose Intentional Actions to Build Life Giving Habits:

- **Daily Surrender of the Past**: Practice releasing past mistakes, regrets, and achievements to God each morning. This opens your heart to new opportunities for growth, freeing you from past limitations as you focus on the upward call of God (Philippians 3:13-14).
- **Set Faith-Filled Goals**: Create goals that align with God's purposes for your life, focusing on spiritual growth, character development, and service to others. Let these goals guide your actions and reinforce your commitment to Kingdom living.
- **Seek God's Presence in Uncertainty**: When faced with challenges, remind yourself of Joshua 1:9. Embrace courage by consciously acknowledging God's presence, praying for strength, and stepping forward in trust rather than fear.
- **Reflect and Adjust**: At the end of each week, reflect on your spiritual journey. Celebrate growth areas, identify where you need more courage, and ask God for guidance. This habit

encourages steady growth and continuous alignment with His Kingdom purposes.

These practices build resilience and a faith-centered mindset, helping you walk forward in alignment with God's will.

- **Immerse in God's Word Daily:** Make it a habit to start or end your day with Scripture, allowing God's Word to renew your mind and direct your actions. Regular immersion in His Word reinforces Kingdom values and strengthens your faith foundation.
- **Surround Yourself with Encouraging Community:** Connect with other believers who are also committed to spiritual growth. Join a small group or accountability partner to share experiences, pray together, and encourage one another as you pursue God's call in your life.

These actions foster a supportive, faith-filled environment that propels you forward in your journey with Christ.

Our Personal 30 Day Journey Conclusion:

This is not the end, just a personal path we've intentionally taken together, along the way of our Life's journey. We *Stay LITT* in Life as we continue to grow in knowledge, truth and relationship with God. We *Stay LITT* in Life when we seek first the Kingdom of God and His righteousness. Embrace our divine identity, follow the King and Live "The Life". Embrace Kingdom Living, Cultivate a Kingdom Culture, Shine & Share His Light as we journey in life.

Our 30 Day Journey Recap:

- We've learned the importance of daily devoted time in connecting with God and understanding His will for our lives.
- We've been reminded of the power of prayer and the peace it brings to our hearts.
- We've discovered the joy and blessing in serving others and the strength found in community.
- We've explored the transformative impact of practicing forgiveness, humility, and patience.
- We've been encouraged to embrace God's rest, wisdom, trusting in His provision and timing.

Embracing Your Place in God's Kingdom

As we wrap up this 30-day journey together, we celebrate not only the steps taken but the lifelong path of growth and transformation that lies ahead. Through this devoted time, you've been invited to seek God wholeheartedly, grounding your life in His Word, pursuing His righteousness, and stepping confidently into your identity as a cherished child of God—an ambassador of His Kingdom, a royal heir among the family of believers. Each day's reflection and practices have given you practical ways to draw closer to the values and heart of God, offering tools to build a life rich in His wisdom, grace, and truth.

Reflecting on all that we have explored, you've had the opportunity to dive into key aspects of living out Kingdom values: trust, love, humility, forgiveness, patience, prayer, and courage. These themes have laid a foundation, but they are only the beginning. Now, the choice is yours. What new steps will you take? How will you live out the truths you've learned about God and His calling over your life?

As you continue in your life's journey, commit to intentionally seeking God's truths, inviting transformation, and cultivating fellowship with Him and other Believers on the same journey. Let the values and teachings of Jesus shape your daily actions, relationships, and decisions to build a Kingdom culture within and around you. Remember, as a Believer, you are a royal child of God, a part of His divine family.

My prayer is that you be stirred to seek and discover God's universal purpose and your unique role in it. May you continue to grow in your priesthood, fellowship and hearing from God. I pray that you answer the call of Kingship while growing in your fellowship and relationship with God, the Father, and Jesus Christ, His appointed King, our King Brother. I pray that you walk in your divine identity, calling and purpose with joy and anticipation. We are on a journey of life. Continue to learn, grow, and live out the values of God's Kingdom, knowing that He is with you every step of the way.

Decide today, what will you plant to establish in your life and what will you water to grow in your life. Decide what you will let go and release as you move forward. What we do will fuel who we become. What will be YOUR NEW? What will YOU CONTINUE in YOUR Journey? Decide today... Then Walk it out as you grow in wisdom.

Consider these to Continue the Journey of Growing Spiritually in Truth, Your Divine Identity, Royalty, Kingdom Community and Faith:

1. **Continuous Learning:** Commit to ongoing study of God's Word. Consider joining a Bible study group or following a Bible reading plan. Consider going back through this devotion yet reading more scriptures around the leading scriptures for more context.

2. **Prayer Life:** Keep cultivating a rich prayer life. Set aside specific times for prayer, but also practice praying continuously throughout the day.

3. **Community Engagement:** Deepen your involvement in a faith community. Fellowship with other believers is essential for encouragement, accountability, and growth.

4. **Serving and Giving:** Look for new opportunities to serve within your community and beyond. Remember, our gifts and actions can have a profound impact on the world around us.

5. **Personal Reflection:** Regularly take time for self-examination and spiritual inventory. Assess areas of growth as well as areas needing attention, bringing them before God in prayer.

From The Author

As we move forward, let's do so with the confidence that comes from knowing we are deeply loved and empowered by God and gifted with The Holy Spirit. Our journey of faith is not a sprint but a marathon, filled with moments of victory, challenge, revelations and profound beauty. Let us press on, holding fast to the Word and promises of God, embracing the adventure of Kingdom living here on Earth.

Words of Truth & Wisdom for your Journey

Learn God's Truth, Practice What You Know, Live What You Learn.

Yahweh so loved the world he gave and desires for all to be saved and know the Truth... to have eternal life, to have life more abundantly.

His will, our choice... All are invited into the family. Our belief is the key to this Family.

As Believers, we are children of God, Children of Love. Learn the King, See the Father. Embrace the guiding, teaching, comfort, reminding and transformation through the Holy Spirit.

Love God with your whole heart, Soul & Strength...
Love yourself, love others. Live the abundant life,
embrace God's Royal Family Kingdom Cultured
Lifestyle.

Learn God's Truth, Increase your Fellowship, Seek first
the Kingdom of God and His Righteousness, Practice
what you know, Live What you learn... Grow in truth,
relationship, belief, faith, trust & GODFIDENCE.

We have access, help, power, authority and grace with
a divine identity and purpose.

We're created for His pleasure and glory.

Share His Love, Shine Your Light & Be the Salt

So whatever you do, do it for the Glory of God.

Reflect his nature and represent the Family Kingdom
Culture by how you see God, fellowship, grow, follow
Jesus and Live.

Love, Light & Salt 🔥

Stay LITT in Life

Embrace the Journey with GODfidence!

~ A Personal Message ~

As I embrace my identity, transformation and calling, I will embrace and honor my God given name. The name that will never change. The name that describes me and the daughter God created and purposed me to be.

As I have journeyed in life, my name has grown and changed. It speaks to my journey, it carries stories, it carries the past, my experiences, lessons, first of many, the best gift, my Merciful Gift of God, the process of equipping me, the healing and preparation for my journey ahead. Monica Renee' Griffin-Monroe, Yes... That is my legal name. A name that tells my story.

Yet, as I am moving with the seasons of my life, I have been blessed with a new life, a new beginning, a found purpose, a Kingdom driven mission, a new me and a new way of living and loving. I am in the second half of my life, the best half and I have decided that I will affectionately go by my God Given birth name, Monica Renee'.

There is so much significance in my name... Today I step into my new life, today I take my place in God's Kingdom, embracing the new me... Loving her immensely. Yahweh is my Heavenly Father. I embrace my adoption. I am my Father's Beloved Daughter.

I am Daddy's Gurl, I am Monica Renee'.

Sharing HIS Love, Shining HIS Light & Being HIS Salt

Love, Light & Salt

Sponsored By:

*Stay*LITT LLC
Stay Leveraging Innovation To
Transform & Thrive

For more information, contact Monica Renee'.
Explore and learn about Stay LITT as we grow and
Stay L.I.T.T. in Life (Stay Living Intentionally to
Transform & Thrive)

- **Email: staylittministries@gmail.com**
- **Social Media:**
    - **TikTok @choosingthekingdom**
    - **Instagram: @Staylittllc**
- **Stay LITT Soul Care Essentials
  www.staylitt.shop**
    - **Emotional Wellness Luxe Candles**
    - **Emotional Wellness Luxe Sprays**
    - **& More**
- **Stay LITT Ministries   www.staylittsoulcare.com**
    - **Stay LITT Safe Sircle Book
      Journey**
    - **Stay LITT Safe Sircle Socials,
      Retreats, Events & Vacations**
- **Stay LITT LLC ~Education Transformation   .
  Solutions**
    - **Instructional Consulting Services**
        - **We are L.I.T.T. We are Leveraging
          Innovation to Transform & Thrive in
          Educational Systems, regardless of
          Setting, including Home Schooling.**
        - **We Enhance Facilitation, Learning
          Outcomes, Collaborative Team
          Teaching and IEP Implementation.**
        - **We are Accommodations,
          Differentiation and Personalized
          Learning Experts.**
        - **We design solutions to organize,
          optimize and manage learning for
          ALL.**
    - **www.staylittllc.com**
    - **monica@staylittllc.com**

www.ingramcontent.com/pod-product-compliance
Lightning Source LLC
Chambersburg PA
CBHW071752120626

46550CB00002B/761